W
f

YAR

D1079260

£1

Best
TEA SHOP WALKS
IN SUFFOLK

Michael Anderton

SIGMA
Leisure

Copyright © Michael Anderton, 1998

All Rights Reserved. No part of this publication may be reproduced, stored in a retrieval system, or transmitted in any form or by any means – electronic, mechanical, photocopying, recording, or otherwise – without prior written permission from the publisher or a licence permitting restricted copying issued by the Copyright Licensing Agency, 90 Tottenham Court Road, London W1P 0LA. This book may not be lent, resold, hired out or otherwise disposed of by trade in any form of binding or cover other than that in which it is published, without the prior consent of the publisher.

Published by Sigma Leisure – an imprint of
Sigma Press, 1 South Oak Lane, Wilmslow, Cheshire SK9 6AR, England.

British Library Cataloguing in Publication Data
A CIP record for this book is available from the British Library.

ISBN: 1-85058-649-7

L942.64

Typesetting and Design by: Sigma Press, Wilmslow, Cheshire.

Cover: River Brett at Hadleigh.

Maps: David Nutall

Photographs: the author

Printed by: MFP Design and Print

NORFOLK LIBRARY AND
INFORMATION SERVICE

SUPP	JARROLD
INV.NO.	3209
ORD DATE	29.10.98

Disclaimer: the information in this book is given in good faith and is believed to be correct at the time of publication. No responsibility is accepted by either the author or publisher for errors or omissions, or for any loss or injury howsoever caused. Only you can judge your own fitness, competence and experience.

Contents

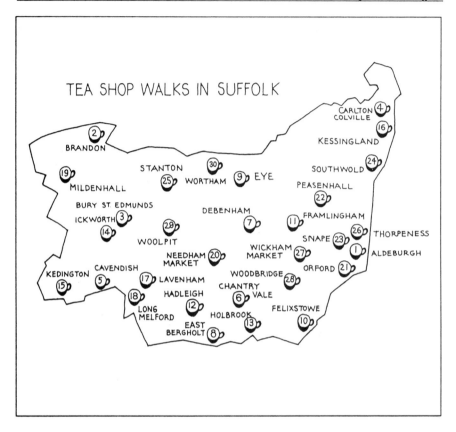

KEY

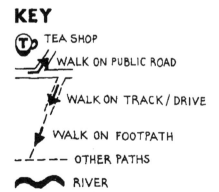

TEA SHOP

WALK ON PUBLIC ROAD

WALK ON TRACK / DRIVE

WALK ON FOOTPATH

———— OTHER PATHS

~~~ RIVER

Suffolk

About the County

Suffolk's countryside provides the walker with a wide range of features to explore, whether it be coastal margin, river valley, central fertile agricultural plateau or the dry sandy Breckland. The broad clear sky merges with the land to provide a scenic landscape patchwork, in a county which inspired John Constable and Thomas Gainsborough, two of England's greatest painters.

There are over 3,500 miles of Public Rights of Way to explore, providing an opportunity to get into the countryside for walks of infinitely varying lengths. For the long distance devotee the county is bounded by a series of promoted routes, the Angles Way along the border with Norfolk, the Coast and Heaths Path down the North Sea coastline, the Stour Valley Path along the border with Essex and a section of the ancient Icknield Way to complete the loop. For the less adventurous there is a network of routes connecting the picturesque and welcoming villages and towns, usually dominated by great churches standing serenely on guard and useful as a point of reference for navigation in the adjoining countryside.

Suffolk's small market towns and villages retain dwellings with their mixture of pink wash, timber frame and flint faced walls, exuding an air of tranquillity to attract visitors from all over the world. However, the past also co-exists harmoniously with the present. The port of Felixstowe is now the largest in the UK and is connected with the industrial Midlands by the A14 trunk road, running east to west as a backbone through the county and an umbilical cord for the port.

New highways such as this are nothing new to the county, the Romans criss-crossed the Suffolk landscape with their straight roads, linking the forts of Camulodinium (Colchester) to Cambretorium (Coddenham) and Caister (Norwich). The lines of these old roads can clearly be seen on maps of the county, many are still in use as the modern routes of today, or have become part of the path network and green lanes radiating out from every village.

Other forms of transportation also figure in Suffolk's past, the rivers Stour, Gipping, Blyth and Lark were all once canalised and navigable to provide a means of importing fuel, timber and manufactured goods. Even the horse manure from the streets of London was brought in by barge to fertilise the land and improve yields. The outward trip down river took away produce such as malt, wheat, sugar beet, hay and straw, even Copralite, fossilised dinosaur dung, was transported by barge, to be ground up and used as fertiliser.

The demise of these navigations was brought about by the development of the railways and the competition that they presented. The age of steam saw another rapid change to the lifestyle of Suffolk, bringing easier travel and cheaper goods to the common country people. Sadly most of the old branch lines have now disappeared and, only in a few places, are the former track beds available for the public to walk along and explore.

Walking in the country

The paths used on these walks are generally on public rights of way but some permissive paths provided by landowners are included. You have a right of way along defined public footpaths, bridleways, byways and roads used as public paths.

Walking boots are recommended for all seasons in order to protect your feet, although walking shoes and trainers are adequate for much of the year. After very wet weather it might be wise to wear wellington boots as some of the paths can get quite muddy. Don't forget to take enough suitable clothing with you. When you are a mile or two from shelter and the heavens open up you will wish you brought that waterproof. It can also get quite chilly in an unexpected breeze or when you are out of the sun.

Remember the Highway Code and walk on the right hand side of the road. However, when you are on the inside of a blind bend, cross over to the other side so that you can be seen a bit sooner.

Always leave gates as you find them; if livestock are controlled by the gate, make sure you close it securely.

The Tea Shops

After a pleasant walk in the countryside what better to way round off your journey than a visit to a welcoming tea shop. Whether it is to warm you up after a winter ramble on a frosty morning, a refreshing drink on a sunny day, sitting in the shade to cool a damp brow or a complete meal to restore your energy for the rest of the day. And what a variety you will find in Suffolk, the tea shops come in all shapes and sizes, the range of buildings where they now operate could be used to produce enough material for another book.

There are tea shops in former cow sheds, barns, thatched cottages, stables, stately homes, antique shops, railway stations and maltings, each one you come across has a new story about its past, providing you with a fascinating memory of your visit.

Many of the tea shops are open all year round although a few are closed during the winter months, it would therefore be wise to telephone in advance to check the latest opening times. The details about each establishment recorded here were checked with proprietors before going to press, but should nevertheless be rechecked before a visit is contemplated.

Finally, please respect the usually spotless tea shops, many of which have fitted carpets. If you are unable to take your muddy boots off, they could easily be covered with a pair of plastic bags carried in the pocket for such emergencies.

Country Code

Enjoy the countryside and respect its life and work.
❖ Guard against all risk of fire.
❖ Fasten all gates.
❖ Keep your dogs under close control.
❖ Keep to public paths across farmland.
❖ Use gates and stiles to cross fences, hedges and walls.
❖ Leave livestock, crops and machinery alone.
❖ Take your litter home.
❖ Help keep all water clean.
❖ Protect wildlife, plants and trees.
❖ Take special care on country roads.
❖ Make no unnecessary noise.

Public Transport

Suffolk County Council provides an excellent public transport information service. By telephoning the TraveLine on 0645 583358 at local call rates from anywhere, up to date details about bus, coach and rail journeys in Suffolk can be obtained. When you call you should have a pen and paper to record the answers and the following information ready about your journey:-

❖ Where you want to travel from
❖ Where you want to travel to
❖ When you want to travel (time and date)
❖ Whether you want to break your journey

The TraveLine hours are:

❖ Monday to Friday: 8.45am to 6pm.
❖ Saturday: 9am to 12.30pm.
❖ Answerphone at all other times

These days the public transport system is in constant change and services come and go overnight. Therefore, only the TraveLine telephone number has been given with each walk.

Ordnance Survey maps

The relevant Ordnance Survey Pathfinder sheet details are given with each walk. However, these will soon be phased out and replaced by the Explorer and Outdoor Leisure series, details of these new maps are therefore given in brackets.

Tourist Information Centres

Aldeburgh TIC, The Cinema, High Street, IP15 5AU. Tel 01728 453637. Easter – Oct: daily 9am – 5.15pm.

Beccles TIC, The Quay, Fen Lane, NR34 9BH. Tel. 0150 2713196. Easter-Oct: daily 9am – 1pm, 2pm – 5pm.

Bury St Edmunds TIC, Angel Hill, IP33 1UZ. Tel 01284 764667. Easter-Oct: Monday – Saturday 9.30am – 5.30pm, Sunday 10am – 3pm, Nov – Easter: Monday – Friday 10am – 4pm, Saturday 10am – 1pm.

Felixstowe TIC, Leisure Centre, Sea Front, IP11 8AB. Tel 01394 276770. Easter – Oct: daily 9am – 5.30pm, Oct – Easter: daily 9am – 5pm except Sunday 10am – 1pm.

Ipswich TIC, St Stephen's Church, St Stephen's Lane, IP1 1DP. Tel 01473 258070. Monday – Saturday 9am – 5pm.

Lavenham TIC, Lady Street, CO10 9RA. Tel 01787 248207. Easter – end Oct: 10am – 4.45pm.

Lowestoft TIC, The East Point Pavilion, Royal Plain NR33 OAF. Tel 01502 523000. Open daily.

Newmarket TIC, Palace House, Palace Street, CB8 8EP. Tel 01638 667200. All year: Monday – Friday 9am – 5pm, Saturday 10am – 1pm.

Southwold TIC, Town Hall, IP18 6EG. Tel 01502 724729. Easter – Oct: daily 10am – 5.30pm.

Stowmarket, Mid Suffolk TIC, Wilkes Way, IP14 1DE. Tel 01449 676800. Easter – Dec: Monday – Friday 9am – 5pm (5.30pm July/Aug), Saturday 9.30am – 4.30pm, Jan – Easter: Monday – Friday 9am – 5pm, Saturday 9.30am – 1.30pm.

Sudbury TIC, Town Hall, Market Hill, CO10 6TL. Tel 01787 881320. Easter – Sept: 10am – 4.45pm, Oct – Easter 10am – 2.45pm.

Woodbridge TIC, Station Buildings, Station Road IP12 4AJ. Tel 01394 382240. Easter – Oct Monday – Friday 9am – 5.30pm, Saturday – Sunday 9.30am – 5pm, Oct – Easter Monday – Friday 9am – 5.30pm, Saturday 10am – 5pm, Sunday 10am – 1pm.

Brandon Information Centre, 31 High Street. Tel. 01842 814955. Monday, Tuesday, Thursday, Friday 8.30am – 2pm, Saturday 9am – 12noon.

Walk 1: Aldeburgh

Route: Fort Green – Slaughden – River Alde – West Row Point – Aldeburgh Marshes – Allotment Gardens – Jubilee Walk – School Road – High Street – Fort Green.

Terrain: Track, river wall path, pasture and road, 5 stiles, sometimes muddy.

Start: Fort Green car park, Slaughden Road, Ordnance Survey map reference TM 464559.

Length: 3½ miles (two short cuts).

Map: Ordnance Survey Pathfinder sheet 1009 Aldeburgh and Orford (Explorer sheet 212).

Public Transport: For details telephone Suffolk County Council's Public Transport Information Travel Line – 0645 583358.

Road Route: From the A12 between Woodbridge and Saxmundham follow A1094 to Aldeburgh. Continue south through the centre of the town to the Fort Green car park off Slaughden Road.

The Tea Shop

Captain's Cabin Restaurant and Tea Rooms, High Street, Aldeburgh IP15 5AQ. Telephone 01728 452520. Proprietor Andrew Moore. Morning coffee is from 10am and 10.30am on Sundays. Lunches from 12noon to 2.15pm. Cream teas served during the afternoon. Other snacks, bacon rolls, baked potatoes, French-fries, filled rolls, side salad etc. Captain's special three course meal chosen from normal menu with a glass of wine and coffee all at a fixed price.

Open daily throughout the year from 10am. Evening meals daily during the summer, suspended during the winter months, but available from 5pm to 7pm at weekends from Easter to November. Seating for 40.

Sea Defences

The sea wall forms a vital sea defence protecting Aldeburgh which since the 16th century has lost 6 streets to the sea on the east of the

Moot Hall, Aldeburgh

town. It has recently been improved at a cost of many millions of pounds, hopefully securing the future of the town. The sea wall, Martello Tower and Sailing Club are all that remains of the village of Slaughden, which was recorded as a harbour in the 1550s. The 16th century Moot Hall at Aldeburgh is the office of Aldeburgh Town Council and houses a museum depicting the town's history, maritime affairs and prints and relics from the Snape Anglo-Saxon ship burial.

The Marshes

The town marshes have been owned by the Aldeburgh Town Council since the 16th century. Today the marshes are leased to a local farmer who manages much of the land by traditional livestock grazing and some is cultivated for arable crops. There are many estuary and marshland birds to be seen with patient observation. The reed-filled dykes are frequented by kingfishers, snipe and reed buntings, while during migration green sandpipers may be seen. In winter the wetter parts of the marsh attract white fronted and brent geese and bewick swans. Short eared owls, hen harriers, sparrow hawks and merlins hunt smaller birds such as meadow pipits and skylarks which frequent the marshes, gorse and bramble scrub. In spring ruff, greenshank and whimbrel may be seen, whilst across the mud flats and on the river look out for herons fishing and other species of wading birds including curlews, redshanks, avocets, godwits, ringed plovers and dunlin.

The Walk

From the Fort Green car park walk south along the sea wall or along the wide stony track to a point just before reaching the car park and Slaughden Sailing Club. Turn right where the path is marked with a footpath sign, passing through a wooden barrier onto the path on top of the river wall, heading inland. This path has had the surface renewed and is along the top of the marsh protection bank with the River Alde on the left. The tall masts to the south belong to the wireless station on Orford Ness, that 10-mile long spit of shingle caused by North Sea drift and dominating the coastline.

At the first bend in the path to the left there is a set of steps down to the right, leading to the first short cut back to the town along an access track if required. Continue along the bank top path on the section of repaired path, which, after it comes to an end, becomes a little muddy in places as it approaches a stile. At a second stile there is another opportunity to turn off right on a short cut path if required. It is marked at the bottom of the bank with a three arm footpath sign to short cut across Aldeburgh Marshes and join up with the walk on the northern section.

Continue to follow the bank top path, by the time you reach stile number three the path has become quite grassy and at stile number four the path suddenly turns sharply right at West Row Point. The town can now be seen ahead, and after about 100 metres, another section of repaired path surface provides easy walking on top of the recently improved river wall.

At the end of this newly surfaced section of path there is a footpath sign before stile number five, turn right down a set of steps and through a number of metal gates into a pasture. This is quite muddy during the winter months but walk along the left edge of the field to the end and a metal gate with a step-less stile. Bear diagonally left across the next pasture, heading in the general direction of the church, which can be seen in the trees on the horizon, to a metal hurdle and footbridge into the next field. Cross this section of pasture, bearing slightly right to another hurdle leading into an arable field.

There is usually a well-worn path across this field to another hurdle and footbridge at the other side giving access to another pasture. Cross this to reach the edge of the allotment gardens, then over two footbridges, to a path through the centre of the vegetable plots and a small wooden gate on the far side leading out to Jubilee Walk.

Turn right along the track between the gardens on the right and the allotments on the left. Follow the lane past the old sewage pumping station and out to School Road. Turn right on the roadside footway, past Aldeburgh County Primary School to the High Street. Turn right along Slaughden Road to return to the start of the walk at Fort Green by the coastguard lookout station.

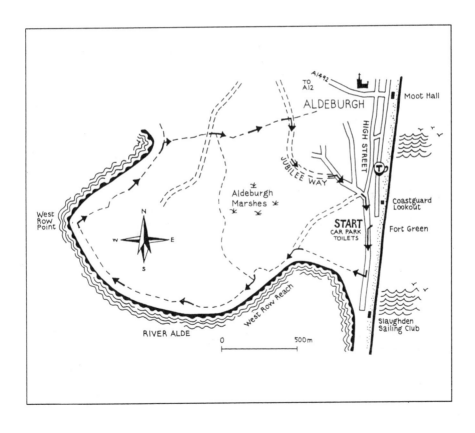

Walk 2: Brandon

Route: Brandon Country Park Visitor Centre – Entrance Drive – Brandon Forest – Mausoleum – Lake – Visitor Centre.

Terrain: Woodland paths and tracks, no stiles or gates.

Start: Brandon Country Park car park – Ordnance Survey map reference TL 785853.

Length: 3 miles (several short cuts on other walks available).

Map: Ordnance Survey Pathfinder sheet 942 Lakenheath and Brandon (Explorer sheet 229).

Public Transport: For details telephone Suffolk County Council's Public Transport Information Travel Line – 0645 583358.

Road Route: From Ipswich on A14 to Bury St Edmunds west interchange, then B1106 following signs to Brandon. Turn left into country park (well signed) on the approach to Brandon village. Free parking at the visitor centre car park.

The Tea Shop

The Brandon Munch House, 11 Stores Street, Brandon IP27 0AA. Telephone 01842 813838. Manageress Beverly Webbe. A small tea room in an old flint building at the rear of the Market Square. Teas, coffees, cappuccino, expresso, decaffeinated and hot chocolate. Sandwiches made to order, rolls, French bread sticks, toasted sandwiches, breakfasts, jacket potatoes, soup, pasties and cakes. Seating for 20.

Opening hours Monday to Saturday 9am to 3.30pm.

Brandon

The north west corner of Suffolk lies within a 370 square mile area of light sandy soil extending up into Norfolk and known as Breckland. Although of poor quality, the land was once covered in deciduous woodland and densely occupied during prehistoric times. With rich deposits of flint in the chalk bedrock it became a major area of flint production, mainly for axes, which were used predominantly to

Brandon Town Sign (Flint Knappers)

clear the land for cultivation. The poor land became open heathland and sparsely populated, with many rabbit warrens thriving in the light soil. The area has now been brought back into productive use through the extensive coverage by Forestry Enterprise conifer plantations. The area around Brandon is known as Thetford Forest Park.

Trade

The town of Brandon was notable for two local exports, flint and fur. The ready supply of rabbit skins from the warrens in the area provided a good supply of the material required to make fur hats and other garments in the town's factories, creating a prominent centre of the fur trade. The town was also the last British home of the gun flint industry. The high quality flint found in the chalk deposits in the area was knapped or dressed to provide flints for market. Flint was not only heavily used as a building material, as can be seen from the facings of the houses in the area, but during the Napoleonic wars the trade was at its height supplying huge quantities of much needed gun flints.

Brandon Country Park

Brandon Country Park was once a small part of the estate of Edward Bliss who acquired the land in 1821. The estate was sold to the Forestry Commission in 1927 and the County Council purchased the section that is now the country park in 1972. It is managed jointly by Suffolk County Council and Forest Heath District Council. Within the park there is a short 1-mile tree trail and, radiating from the park, there are four walks of varying lengths into the forest. The park is normally open during daylight hours, usually 8.30am to dusk in summer

The Country Park is the ideal place to see some of the wildlife of the area, birds such as jays, long-tailed tits and even feral golden pheasants and many animals including squirrel, deer, and in summer, adders. The walled garden was once the kitchen garden for Brandon Park House and was opened to the public in 1989. Restoration work has now been completed by laying out the inside of the garden to include a butterfly shrub area, herb and wildflower borders and a pond. It is also suitable for wheel chair access, as are most areas of the park.

The Park Visitor Centre has a distinctive squirrel weathervane and is open April to September 10am to 5pm Monday to Friday and 10am to 5.30pm Saturday and Sunday, October to March 10am to 4pm every day. Facilities include an exhibition about the history and natural history of Breckland, Brandon and the Country Park, walk trail leaflets, maps, souvenirs, confectionery, drinks and ice cream, public toilets.

The Walk

This walk uses parts of the park trails waymarked through the trees, described on the leaflets available from the visitor centre and defined with the letters A to D. From the car park at the front of the visitor centre and picnic area follow the tree trail from the brown and white marker No. 1 on the right, through the trees to the start of walks C and D, marked with a sign, just inside the entrance to the park by the gate and to the rear of the Warden's House.

Follow the wide shady path through the trees, crossing a track and on to a junction of tracks. Turn right on walk C along a wide open track where walk D continues on. Follow route C through a wide cleared area where there is a good example of the timber cultivation

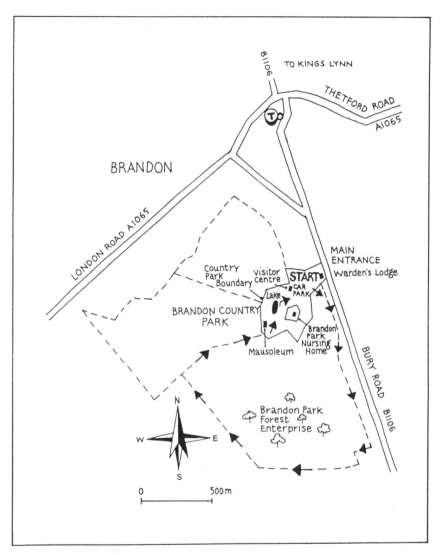

process. To the right there are the young whips that have been planted in furrows, on the left more mature trees of about 2 metres in height and in the background the majestic tall pines ready for felling. At intervals there are stacks of felled timber ready to be carted off to the sawmill.

At the next junction of tracks the walk bears right between the tall trees and then at the next junction, turns right where the route is joined by route B. Follow the track, which soon bears right as a grassy path through the trees, but look out for the Mausoleum in the trees on the left. The Mausoleum was built by Edward Bliss, he was interred here in 1845, although his remains were removed to Brandon churchyard earlier this century. The building has recently been renovated to its original appearance by Suffolk County Council.

From the Mausoleum follow the tree trail if you have the leaflet or take the path past the Mausoleum and lake to return to the car park and the start of the walk. Brandon Park House stands across the lawn and was built by Edward Bliss in 1826, originally with 21 bedrooms. More recently it was used as a hotel from 1987, but from 1993 it has become Brandon Park House Nursing Home.

Walk 3: Bury St Edmunds

Route: Abbey Gate – Cathedral – Honey Hill – Shire Hall – Kevelaer Way – The Crankles – No Man's Meadows – Rougham Road – River Lark – Kevelar Way – Abbey Gardens – Abbey Gate.

Terrain: Roadside footway, field path and track. Easy walking. The section through the Abbey Gardens is closed at night.

Start: The Abbey Gate at Angel Hill, Ordnance Survey map reference TL 855642.

Length: 2 miles (one short cut).

Map: Ordnance Survey Pathfinder sheet 984 Bury St Edmunds and Woolpit (Explorer sheet 211A).

Public Transport: For details telephone Suffolk County Council's Public Transport Information Travel Line – 0645 583358.

Road Route: Bury St Edmunds is just off the A14 between Ipswich (25 miles) and Newmarket. Follow brown tourist signs to town centre. Plenty of pay and display car park sites in the town.

Tea Shop

The Courtyard Café, Manor House Museum, Honey Hill, Bury St Edmunds IP33 1HF. Telephone 01284 725209. Proprietor Abbey Leisure Services Catering Services, Manager Andrew McGowan, Supervisor Jane Mudd. A wide variety of home made cakes, sponges, scones and cheese scones, toasted tea cakes, sandwiches, filled baguettes, variety of teas, coffee, café au lait, decaffeinated coffee, chocolate, orange juice and soft drinks. Daily specials on the blackboard including home made pastas and continental salads, sweet and savoury snacks and jacket potatoes. Ice Creams and crisps. Seating for 20 – 30 with extra seats in the courtyard during the summer. Smoking outside in Courtyard.

Opening Monday to Saturday 10am to 5pm, Sunday 10.30am to 4.30pm. The café is adjoining the museum's gift shop.

Abbey Gardens, Bury St Edmunds

Bury St Edmunds

The town was known in the Saxon period as Beodric's Worth and had a monastery established by King Sigbert in around 630. Bury St Edmunds takes its name from Edmund the East Anglian Anglo-Saxon king who was killed at Hoxne in 869 by the invading Danes. He was subsequently canonised and his remains were interred in the church. In the 11th century, the town became established around the Abbey and for 600 years a shrine to which pilgrims flocked. The Abbey became very rich and one of the largest and most influential in the country. The barons of England met here in 1214 in order to force King John to sign the Magna Carta. The motto on the crest of the town means 'shrine of the King, cradle of the law' thus recognising these two events. The huge Abbey was dismantled following the dissolution by Henry VIII, the ruins that remain in the attractive Abbey Gardens now provide a unique historic park for relaxation and to explore. It is possible to trace the mediaeval sites of the cloisters, refectory, cellarer's apartment and the chapter house.

The Crankles and No Man's Meadows

No Man's Meadows and the Crankles have an interesting history, dating back to the abbey of St Edmundsbury. It appears that the area was created artificially in the medieval period as a result of diverting the course of the River Linnet in order to provide a millstream for the abbey. The meadows would have been used for grazing livestock, whilst it is thought that the Crankles was where the Abbey fish-ponds were situated, and where fish such as bream, tench and pike might have been bred. The unusual names of 'No Man's Meadows' and 'The Crankles' are quite old, both are used in Thomas Warren's map of 1747. It appears that the area has always been wet and prone to flooding and at different times in the past 300 years drains have been dug across the meadows in an effort to control the water level. The Crankles was also used as pasture land until relatively recently when it was planted with cricket bat willows.

The Walk

From the Abbey Gate on Angel Hill turn left and walk along George Street, past the Cathedral, and on to St Mary's Church on the corner of Honey Hill. Turn left down towards the Shire Hall, where the tea shop can be found on the right of the road in the Manor House Museum. Bear left of the Magistrates Court opposite, to the pedestrian and cycle path at the rear marked to Moreton Hall Estate.

This path crosses the Shire Hall staff car park and on to a bridge over the River Linnet at the start of Kevelar Way. After crossing the river turn right through a wooden barrier along the circular walk path, by an information board. Walk through the cricket bat willows in The Crankles and continue on into No Mans Meadows. These two adjoining areas between the Rivers Lark and Linnet have very different characters, the Crankles is a willow plantation whilst No Man's Meadows are four low-lying water meadows separated by ditches. The two areas are leased to St Edmundsbury Borough Council who manage the land as a local nature reserve open for walking and informal recreation.

Follow the path along the river bank to a footbridge and steps on the right up to the path on the other bank. Note the two large Black Poplar trees on the left, their knobbly trunks contrasting with the tall Lombardy Poplars on the right. The path soon joins a track leading down past the Bury St Edmunds Rugby Football Club, through the

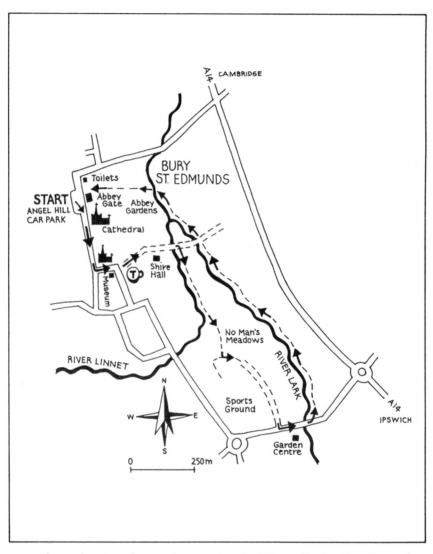

car park, and out to the road opposite the Wyevale Garden Centre on Rougham Road.

Turn left on the roadside foot-way past the entrance to the Mobil garage and after crossing the River Lark, turn left on a bridleway between the river bank and a fenced off field. Follow this path along the river bank to Kevelar Way. The river banks and ditches are particularly important for wetland plants including bur-reed, mead-owsweet, purple loosetrife, water forget-me-not and water mint. Meadowsweet comes from an older name, medesweete, which was used because it flavoured the Anglo-Saxon drink, mede, made of fermented honey. Dragonflies can sometimes be seen darting above the water, but moorhens are more commonly seen. Their short bills are adapted for a broad diet, and the white underneath the tails is used as a threat during, the breeding season.

Cross over Kevelar Way to the tarmac path leading to the Abbey Gardens. At the first junction bear left to the iron bridge over the River Lark then right at the other side. At the next junction turn left up the main drive through the beautiful gardens to return to the start of the walk at the Abbey Gate. There is much to see in the gardens and an extension of the route to see the ruins of the abbey and the superbly maintained gardens will round off your walk perfectly.

Walk 4: Carlton Colville

Route: Burnt Hill Lane – Sprat's Water – Share Marsh – Share Mill – River Waveney – White Cast Marsh – Burnt Hill Lane.

Terrain: Mostly flat, wheelchair friendly kissing gates on easy access route, bridge and steps at River Waveney, could be muddy, several stiles.

Start: Suffolk Wildlife Trust Visitor Centre, Burnt Hill Lane, Carlton Marshes, Ordnance Survey map reference TM 508920.

Length: 3 miles (several short cuts), easy access route 800 metres.

Map: Ordnance Survey Pathfinder sheet 925, Lowestoft and Beccles (North) (Outdoor Leisure sheet 40).

Public Transport: For details telephone Suffolk County Council's Public Transport Information Travel Line – 0645 583358.

Road Route: Carlton Marshes Nature Reserve is between Lowestoft and Carlton Colville on the A146 Beccles Road.

Tea Shop

The Crooked Barn Restaurant, Ivy House Farm, Ivy Lane, Oulton Broad, Lowestoft NR33 8HY. Telephone 01502 501353 Fax 01502 501539. Proprietor Caroline Sterry.

In the Conservatory or the sitting room relax and choose from a selection of dishes. Morning coffee is served between 10am and 12noon. A cafetiere of coffee, a portion of home-made gateaux or other snacks are available. There is a bistro luncheon menu in the Crooked Barn Restaurant (no smoking) a three course meal from the table d'hôte menu includes coffee.

Afternoon tea is served in the conservatory or sitting-room where a selection of home-made gateaux, cakes, toast and sandwiches are available. A wide range of teas and coffees are stocked and bookings can be taken in advance. Seating is also available in the courtyard and garden during fine weather. For Sunday lunch there is roast lunch in addition to the bistro menu.

Seating in Conservatory and sitting room 20. All dishes are made on the premises.

Category 1 rating from Tourist Board for disabled access. Bed and

The Crooked Barn Restaurant, Carlton Marshes

breakfast in the country house style accommodation, and catering for luncheon buffets and parties.

Carlton Marshes

The marsh lies within the Broads National Park although the car park and visitor centre are owned by Suffolk Wildlife Trust. Water levels on the east coast have changed considerably over the centuries, during Roman times the area would have been a wide estuary of reed and salt marsh. Major drainage has been taking place since the 18th century and prior to this the annual cycle of vegetation growing and dying created vast reed beds with trees only growing on the higher ground. As a result of drainage, vast areas of peat lying on top of the clay soil were created, providing a source of fuel for the marshmen who lived here. Some of the diggings have been found to be 5 metres deep, the resulting holes filling with water to become the Broads that are used for recreation today.

The Walk

This circular walk begins at the Suffolk Wildlife Trust's Visitor Centre on Carlton Marshes. Part of the route has been developed as an easy access trail and the gates can be easily opened from a wheelchair. A short specially surfaced trail provides an ideal opportunity for people with mobility difficulties to experience the sights and sounds to be found on the marsh. Following the main route, the path passes through a landscape of arable fields, river and pastures, intersected by drainage dykes where wildlife flourishes.

Follow the continuation of Burnt Hill Lane down from the Visitor Centre to a gate and then left over the stile. People with disabilities may use the small gate at the side, please ask at the Visitor Centre if you need help. Turn left through the kissing gate and follow the surfaced path as it winds along the left edge of a grazing marsh. Look out for a turning to the left where the easy access route circles Sprats Water, Round Water, and through an area of fen before rejoining the main path.

Pass through a number of gates and stile combinations to the next junction, marked with an information board and map of the marsh, and at the point where the easy access path rejoins. Turn north on a grassy track, first curving round to the left to a field gate and then sharply right following a line of electricity poles, straight towards the River Waveney at Share Mill. The power line provides electricity for the drainage pumps, which control the water levels on the marsh.

At the ruins of the mill bear left to a metal foot-bridge over the dyke and up steps to join the Angles Way footpath on the bank of the river. There is a fine view from the river wall across the marshes towards the Visitor Centre and across the busy river into Norfolk. Turn right along the riverside path for about 250 metres to a point where a fence is placed across the river bank. Turn right down a few steps to a field edge path and on to a short section of track. Where the track bears left, turn right over a stile, marked with a footpath sign, and into a pasture. Turn left and head for the gate that can be seen on the other side.

Pass through a series of cattle control barriers to reach the track again. For a short cut continue straight ahead along the main track on the easy route back to the Visitor Centre. To continue the main walk turn left after the cattle control barriers, up to the path along-

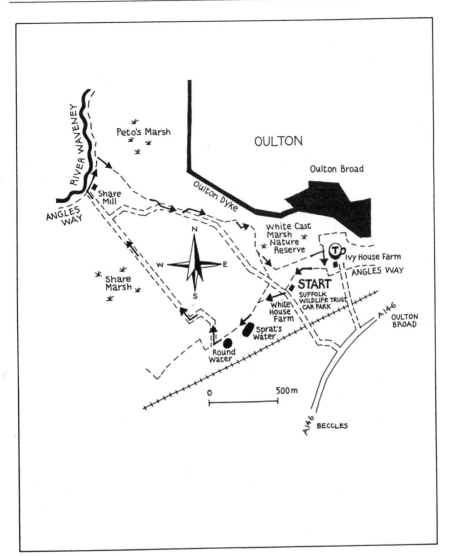

side White Cast Marsh Nature Reserve. This route is marked with another public footpath sign post directing walkers right along the top of the embankment. Follow the well-worn path through the bushes, crossing two stiles and on along the edge of the marsh on the raised path.

After a long straight the raised path turns left to continue along the river embankment at the edge of the reserve. Look out for a concrete sluice on the river side of the path, at a point close to the trees at the rear of Ivy House Farm. Turn right on the path away from the river and along the side of the trees to reach a pasture. To walk to the Ivy House Farm Restaurant turn left to the drive and entrance.

To return to the Visitor Centre, turn right with the dyke on the right, following the path in the pasture back to the car park and the start of the walk.

Walk 5: Cavendish

Route: Cavendish High Street – River Stour – Dismantled Railway and Station – Water Lane – Blacklands Farm – Ducks Hall – Cavendish Church – The Green – The High Street.

Terrain: Well defined field edge and cross field paths, tracks and road, one stile.

Start: Cavendish High Street, The George PH, Ordnance Survey map reference TL805465.

Length: 3 miles (one short cut).

Map: Ordnance Survey Pathfinder sheet 1029 Sudbury and Lavenham (Explorer sheet 196).

Public Transport: For details telephone Suffolk County Council's Public Transport Information Travel Line – 0645 583358.

Road Route: From Ipswich on A1071 and A134 to Long Melford then A1092 to Cavendish.

The Tea Shop

Sue Ryder Foundation Tea Room and Museum, High Street, Cavendish CO10 8AY. Telephone 01787 280252. For bookings contact Mrs Baxter. Cream teas, set teas, sandwiches, wide range of home made cakes, snacks, hot lunches, roast on Sunday.

Open all year daily 10am to 5.30pm except Christmas Day. Seating for 90, no smoking, wheelchair access. Museum 80p for adults and 40p for children. Well stocked gift shop.

Cavendish

The picture postcard scene of the almshouses and 14th century church across Cavendish Green is one of those views that feature on chocolate boxes, calendars and many of the tourist guides of Suffolk. The old thatched buildings of the village and the Sue Ryder Foundation Museum attract great interest and a constant flow of visitors is always to be seen. The name of the village stems from the former lords of the manor, Sir John Cavendish was also at one time

Cavendish - The Green

the Lord Chief Justice of England. It was his son John Cavendish who killed the leader of the peasants revolt, Wat Tyler, in 1381. But the peasants caught up with him and beheaded him in Bury St Edmunds Market Place.

The Walk

Start from The George public house, opposite the Sue Ryder Foundation Museum and Tea Room, close to The Green. Walk along the High Street past The Bull public house and Cavendish Post Office. The street was once part of the Roman road network although it is unclear if there was ever a Roman settlement here.

Turn right on a narrow footpath, marked with a sign post, between the pale pink Western House and Granby Cottages. Follow the path between fences and walls to a small gate giving access to a garden. Head through another gate in the fence opposite and turn left under the trees to a footbridge. In the pasture on the other side bear left diagonally over the raised embankment of the former railway track to a line of poplar trees. Turn left along the other side of the trees, paral-

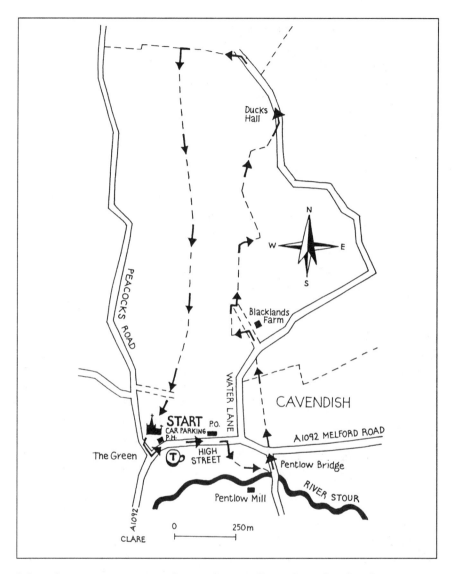

lel to the River·Stour, with Pentlow Mill on the other bank in Essex. At the end of the pasture cross a stile to Pentlow Lane.

Turn left over the former railway crossing, noting the old railway buildings on either side. The station was to the right where a section of platform can be seen. During the 1950s there were five trains a day along this section of the line connecting Haverhill with Long Melford. The line finally closed in 1967.

At the Melford Road, cross straight over to the tarmac path to the left of the Memorial Hall, walking up to the playing field. Cross the field on the embankment separating the cricket pitch from the football pitch, to a gap in the hedge opposite. Cross the next field on a well defined path through the crop and then alongside a hedge to a gap leading out onto Water Lane.

Turn right for about 20 metres on the lane and then left on the concrete drive to Blacklands Farm, as far as the first set of gates. Turn left on a track between trees and wire fence to the corner, then right along the fence to the next corner and right again to reach a track.

Turn left up the wide mown strip to the right of the trees, to a large oak tree at the top, then turn right and follow the edge of the field down to the corner by a deep water course. Turn left along the field edge and water course, following this out to the lane at Ducks Hall.

Turn left up the lane, after a house called September Cottage, the track bears left and, at a gate, turn left through the trees. Turn right along the field edge, following a line of electricity poles, at the first junction of wires turn left on a well defined crop break strip, up over the hill, still following electricity poles.

At the brow of the hill there is a good view across the Stour Valley, of Cavendish Church to the right and Pentlow Tower on the other side of the valley to the left. On the brow of the second hill, Cavendish village comes into view, continue on the path down hill, still following the electricity poles. Near the village the path is lined with young oak trees that have been topped to avoid obstructing the wires overhead.

At the rear gardens of the houses continue on to a crossing track and a staggered barrier across the path. This path leads between fences and walls to a footbridge giving access into the churchyard. St Mary's Church dates from around 1300 when the tower and lower parts of the aisle walls were built. A small room was fitted out in the tower for a priest to live in, with a fireplace and chimney.

Bear right around the church tower to the gate out to Peacocks Road near the Five Bells public house. Turn left, with The Green on the right, down to the High Street and then left to return to the start of the walk at The George Inn on the main street.

Walk 6 : Chantry Vale

Route : Chantry Park – Hadleigh Road – Chantry Vale – Sproughton Church Lane – Sproughton – Gipping Valley River Path – River Gipping – Yarmouth Road – Hadleigh Road – Chantry Park.

Terrain: Mainly river side path and roadside footway, very easy – 5 stiles.

Start : Chantry Mansion off Hadleigh Road, Ipswich, Ordnance Survey map reference TM 138442.

Length : 4½ miles (no short cuts).

Map : Ordnance Survey Pathfinder sheet 1030 Ipswich and Hadleigh (Explorer sheet 197).

Public Transport : For details telephone Suffolk County Council's Public Transport Information Travel Line – 0645 583358.

Road Route : From Ipswich turn left off A1071 Hadleigh Road at the main entrance to Chantry Park, follow signs to free car park.

Tea Shop

Sue Ryder Foundation Stables Coffee Shop and Restaurant, Chantry Park, Hadleigh Road Ipswich IP2 0BP. Telephone 01473 218611. General Manager Doreen Savage, Head Chef Jason Elmer. This uniquely restored old stable block has the original brick floor and hay racks still intact with the tables set out in the stalls, serving morning coffee, lunches, afternoon tea and set high tea. Home made cakes, sandwiches, baguettes and jacket potatoes with a variety of fillings, hot drinks, ice cream. Wide range of tea flavours. Three course table d'hôte menu, salad platters, wine licence, seating for up to 60 people. Choice of menus for large parties and evening functions.

Easy disabled access throughout, no smoking, no dogs except guide dogs.

Opening hours 10am to 4.30pm daily. Other facilities, Gift Shop and Dress Shop.

Former School, Sproughton

Chantry Park

Chantry Park was the home of many notable people for 300 years, in 1927 the estate was sold for housing development. Sir Arthur Churchman, later Lord Woodbridge, purchased it from the developer and gave it to Ipswich Corporation as a gift to be held in permanent trust for the people of Ipswich. From 1945 until the late 1980s many hundreds of people convalesced in Chantry Mansion after hospital treatment and more recently it has become a Sue Ryder nursing home.

The word Chantry is derived from the French word chanter to sing and has its roots in the Latin word cantare. The 50-hectare park is ideal for both passive and active recreation and a haven for both flora and fauna. There are delightful formal garden areas, which vary from colourful bedding displays to flowering shrubs and roses, and landscape features like the cedar trees and well maintained lawns and hedges.

River Gipping

The river was used for transportation as early as the 12th century and work started soon after 1790 to construct a navigation of 17 miles from Ipswich to Stowmarket.

The improved waterway was opened in 1793 and lifted barges 27 metres through 15 locks over its length. The barges were 18 metres long and 4 metres wide and carried 30 tonnes of cargo ranging from slate, coal and timber to manure, chemicals and gun cotton. A railway company leased the navigation in 1846, promptly raised the tolls and failed to carry out maintenance in order to encourage use of the railway.

The canal company regained control of the navigation, but in such poor condition that barges found it hard to reach Stowmarket. Steam tugs were able to operate up to the Fisons works at Papermill Lane, Bramford until 1929. But sadly the canal company went into liquidation and the navigation was ended by an act of parliament in 1932.

The river today still bears the signs of its industrial past with evidence of tow paths, locks and the once predominant water mills that still stand sentry along its length.

The Walk

From the front of Chantry Mansion return down the main drive and through the main gate to the Hadleigh Road. Turn left and cross to the roadside footway for about 300 metres to a footpath on the right, marked with green metal footpath signs. Follow this between fences and hedges to a stile and on between hedges to the end at a second stile.

Cross a short muddy section where the cattle cross between fields to another stile and on along a field edge path with the hedge on the right. At Sproughton Church Lane turn right towards the A14 and, where the lane bends sharply right to the sewage works, take the tarmac path down 14 wide steps to a tunnel under the road.

On emerging at the other side, continue along Church Lane, walking out to Lower Street by the church. Turn right and cross the River Gipping and right again over a stile in the roadside fence along the Gipping Valley River Path. This is the Stowmarket to Ipswich footpath along the tow path of the former navigation.

Look out for the willow pollards along the way, trees that have

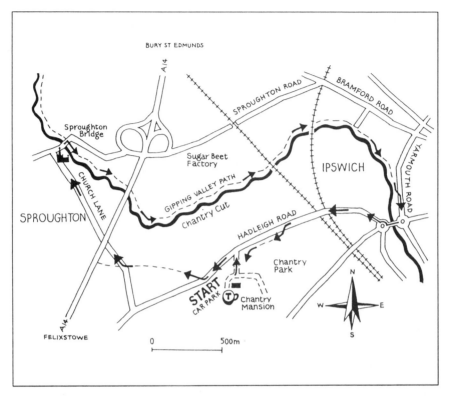

been grown from willow posts set at intervals in the bank which have taken root, sprouted branches and grown into new trees. Follow the river bank path towards Ipswich, at the Anglian Water intake station pass under the arch to the left and return to the river path on the other side. This pumping station extracts water from the river to supply Alton Reservoir where the river water is purified and used to supply Ipswich and the surrounding area. The next feature on the path is the A14 road bridge where the path passes underneath the speeding traffic. The path now passes close to the rear of the sugar beet factory, the odour of the steam from the chimneys is often very strong and sickly when the wind is blowing from the north.

Eventually the path becomes partially surfaced with stone, is less muddy in wet weather and soon passes one of the flood control gates, which are a feature of any walk along the River Gipping. The path next passes under the first railway bridge, this is the main line to Norwich and Bury St Edmunds. Then to a large flood control gate which can be negotiated by turning left up a set of concrete steps to return you to the river path on the other side. The second railway bridge is the branch line to Felixstowe and Lowestoft via Westerfield.

At River Side Road there is access to Bramford Road if required. Continue on along the edge of the river as far as you can go, to the point where the path reaches the Yarmouth Road and the junction of the river and the canal cut under the road, linking with the Alderman Canal. Turn left up the steps to the roadside footway and then right to the traffic lights at the cross-roads. Turn right to the next set of traffic lights at the next cross roads and right up Hadleigh Road, passing the Ranleigh Cycle Warehouse, the Earl Kitchener pub and on over the railway bridge towards Chantry Park.

At Hyntle Close cross the road and enter the park at the corner by an information board. Turn right on the path meandering between the trees bordering the Hadleigh Road, to the main entrance gates, then left up the drive. Turn right in front of the mansion to return to the start of the walk at the car park or to visit the Stables Coffee Shop.

Walk 7: Debenham

Route: Cross Green – High Street – Water Lane – Priory Lane – Pages Mill – Kenton Road – Hill Farm – Crows Hall – River Deben – Winston Road – Winston Church – Ipswich Road – Low Road – Community Centre – Gracechurch Street – Derrybrook Farm – The Butts – Chancery Lane – High Street – Cross Green.

Terrain: Good footpaths, tracks and road, one cross field section, no stiles.

Start: Cross Green car park, Debenham, Ordnance Survey map reference TM 175631.

Length: 5½ miles.

Map: Ordnance Survey Pathfinder sheet 985 Debenham and Bacton (Explorer sheet 211B).

Public Transport: For details telephone Suffolk County Council's Public Transport Information TraveLine – 0645 583358.

Road Route: From Ipswich 11 miles north on B1077 or from Eye 6 miles south on B1077. Free parking on Cross Green car park and other areas within the village.

Tea Shop

The Farmer's Table Cafe, 74 High Street, Debenham IP14 6QP. Telephone 01728 861600. Proprietor Mim Self. Selection of teas in pots, coffee, hot chocolate, milk shakes, soft drinks, ice cream. Afternoon tea, good selection of home made cakes, sandwiches with granary or white bread. Hot snacks on toast, jacket potatoes, ploughman's.

All day breakfast, omelettes. Daily specials on menu board. Home made soups, main courses and desserts. Seats 22 plus garden during summer. No smoking, licensed.

Open Wednesday to Sunday 10am to 5pm (7 days a week in summer and some restrictions in the winter).

Alternative tea shop (50 metres) – The Teapot Pottery, Low Road, Debenham. Telephone 01728 861110. Proprietor Tony Carter.

Watch the highly skilled staff making collectable tea pots. Tea served in courtyard – weather permitting

Opening hours Monday to Friday 9am to 5pm, Saturdays and Bank holidays 10.30am to 4.30pm, Sunday (Easter to Christmas) 2pm to 5pm.

Market Cross, Debenham

The River Deben

The river rises west of Debenham taking water draining from the former wartime airfield at Mendlesham, this is the plateau of middle Suffolk, the ground here is 55 metres above sea level. As the water trickles down towards Debenham it passes along Stony Lane, a public road on the bed of the river where it is actually possible to walk or drive down the River Deben by car. After passing through the centre of Debenham, the river meanders through the countryside in a shallow valley where beds of osiers are grown for basket making, a craft that is still practised in the area.

Debenham

The village clearly takes its name from the river, evidence that the Romans were here have been found in excavations on Priory Field. The Domesday Book of 1086 mentions many people in Debenham and it appears to have been one of the most heavily populated parts of Suffolk. One well-known former resident named his chain of high street shops Debenhams, after the place where he grew up. This unspoilt country village has many picturesque buildings from as early as the 14th century and was chosen as Architectural Village of the Year in 1975.

The Walk

From the Cross Green car park opposite the village sign, walk up through the village on the roadside footway, passing the former Ancient Order of the Foresters Chapel, now an antiques shop which featured in the Lovejoy TV series. After passing the Angel and Red Lion pubs, turn right on Water Lane. If the road is flooded, continue a little further along the street and turn right after the main bridge, on a path at the side of the houses. The ford in Water Lane is the bed on the infant River Deben and can become quite deep after heavy rain.

After Tean House take the left fork on a narrow lane and left up the side of the allotments and a wide grass strip to the top of the field. At the top of the field pass through a gap in the hedge, then along the left edge of the next two fields, to reach the Kenton Road at Pages Mill. Turn left along the road and walk as far as the first left bend, turning off right on the track at Hill Farm.

Follow the track through the farm to the first junction of tracks and turn right, off the circular walk, following the main track as it zigzags around the field edges and down to another junction of tracks. Turn right up between the trees to reach Crows Hall Road opposite Crows Hall Cottages. Turn left along the oak-lined drive towards Crows Hall. Please note that this 16th century moated residence is a private house.

Just before the farm buildings turn right on the track close to the bungalow, walking now down into the Deben Valley. At the road turn right for about 100 metres and then left to a bridge over the river. Note the beds on the left which are used to grow osiers for manufacturing baskets and cane ware locally. Follow the track to the

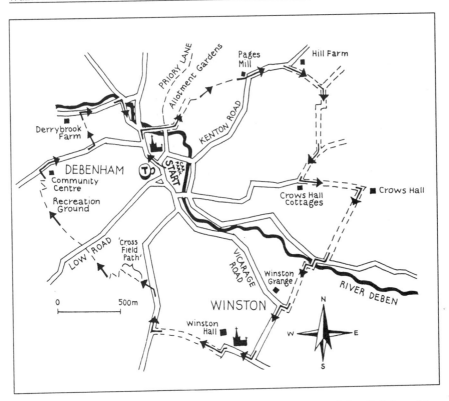

right and then left up the hill, keeping to the right of the field and ignore the left turn to reach the top; turn right out to the B1077 Winston Road.

Turn left, taking great care of the approaching traffic and using the verge where necessary. At the sharp left bend ahead, turn right to pass St Andrews Church, follow the road left around the bend at the end, past the entrance to Winston Hall. Turn right on the track at the left side of a Dutch barn, following this down and then up to the Ipswich Road. Turn right, again taking great care of the speeding traffic, and walk as far as a pink bungalow called Sunny View.

Turn left on the bridleway across the field, heading for a gap in the hedge and small bridge on the far side. In the next field, follow the wide grass path as it zigzags around the edge of the field and down to Low Road. Turn left and then right over a footbridge with white railings, walking up the well-defined field edge to a playing field. Follow the left edge of the field, around the site of a former windmill and out to the road between wire fences or at the side of the Community Hall if preferred.

Turn right along the roadside footway past the High School, and along Gracechurch Street. Turn left at the side of house No. 56 through a wide gateway, following the field edge path down to Derrybrook Farm where the osiers are used to produce a variety of items. Turn right along Derrybrook Lane and the Butts, then right along Chancery Lane to reach the High Street opposite Water Lane.

Turn right through the centre of the village to return to the start of the walk at the Cross Green car park.

Walk 8: East Bergholt

Route: Red Lion pub – John Constable's Studio – Cemetery Lane – Dead Lane – Fen Bridge – River Stour – Flatford – Dazeley's Lane – Brantham Road – Orvis Lane – Flatford Lane – Burnt Oak – St Mary's Church and Bell Cage – Village Centre – Red Lion pub.

Terrain: Road, track pasture, field edge and riverside, 12 stiles, muddy at times.

Start: Red Lion pub and free car park, Ordnance Survey map reference TM 069346.

Length: 5 miles (several short cuts).

Map: Ordnance Survey Pathfinder sheet 1053 Manningtree and Dedham (Explorer sheet 196).

Public Transport: For details telephone Suffolk County Council's Public Transport Information TraveLine – 0645 583358.

Road Route: From A12 or A137 on B1070 road to East Bergholt village centre and Red Lion pub free public car park.

The Tea Shop

The Haywain, Burnt Oak, East Bergholt CO7 6TJ. Telephone 01206 299194. Proprietor Mrs Stella Hyland.

Home made cakes and scones, sandwiches served with garnish. A choice of teas, coffees, soft drinks and alcohol. Bread and salads etc. from local tradesmen. Lunches – soup, salads served with new potatoes, French bread, or bread and butter, snacks on toast, jacket potatoes with side salad, sweets with cream or ice cream. Seating for 14, plus summer seating in the garden.

Opening Hours – Summer 10.30am to 5pm, Winter 10.30am to 4pm, closed Monday and Tuesday and January, February and March.

Alternative Tea Shop

Bridge Cottage Tea Room, Flatford. Telephone 01206 298260. Owned by The National Trust, Manager Katherine King.

Opening Hours – May to September daily 10am to 5.30pm, March, April and October Wednesday to Sunday 11am to 5.30pm, November, Wednesday to Sunday 11am to 3.30pm, December limited opening, closed January and February.

East Bergholt

Situated in the Stour Valley, this was the birthplace of the great landscape painter John Constable RA, it was in this neighbourhood that he painted many of his famous pictures. Flatford Mill, Valley Farm, the dry dock and Willy Lott's Cottage are the scenes of his most famous paintings. Flatford Mill is now a study centre for artists and naturalists. The scenes depicted so richly in John Constable's paintings are renowned throughout the world, born in 1776, he died in 1837 and is buried in Hampstead Cemetery. The Thatched Cottage by the bridge is now owned by the National Trust and contains an exhibition of Constable's life and times.

The church of St Mary's has an unfinished tower, probably as a result of the decline in the wool trade in the 16th century. The bells in-

Flatford Bridge, East Bergholt

tended for the tower are housed in a 400 year old low wooden bell cage in the churchyard. This provides a spectacle for the many visitors who flock to the area, especially when the campanologists are at work and pushing the bells over by hand.

River Stour

The work of making the river open to navigation was started in 1708 with the construction of thirteen wooden locks and a basin and warehouses at the terminus in Sudbury. Barges constructed in the dry dock at Flatford, carrying cargoes of up to 13 tonnes, were pulled by horses between the Cattawade Barrage and Sudbury. Below the barrage the barges were floated on the tide down to Mistley. Barge traffic continued until 1928 when the last barge is recorded up to Dedham Mill.

The Walk

Set off from the free public car park behind the Red Lion pub and turn right via the Post Office to Cemetery Lane. A plaque on a blue and white building in the lane marks John Constable's studio of 1802. The route continues along the lane, through a gate and down the left side of a pasture, to a stile and footbridge at the bottom. Bear right to the path up the right edge of the field ahead. At the top of the rise there are splendid views across the river valley, the churches of Dedham (left) and Stratford (ahead) can easily be identified.

At the path junction at Dead Lane turn left at a sign marked to Dedham Road, down an enclosed path to the end of Donkey Lane, and then left along the valley floor to Fishpond Wood. The path goes right then left, between a fence and the wood, to a stile. Follow the fence and hedge in the pasture, first on the right and then on the left, to another stile and a field edge path. Over two more stiles to Fen Lane and the first opportunity for a short cut up to the left.

Turn right along the lane, over a wide cart bridge and then the new footbridge across the river. A sign announces that Flatford is along the bank to the left. The wide open pasture of the flood plain provides easy walking, there are swans, geese, coots, moorhens and many other birds to identify on the way. At Flatford, cross the bridge by the Thatched Cottage, for a short cut follow the lane up to the left.

Turn right along the road towards Flatford Mill, passing the old

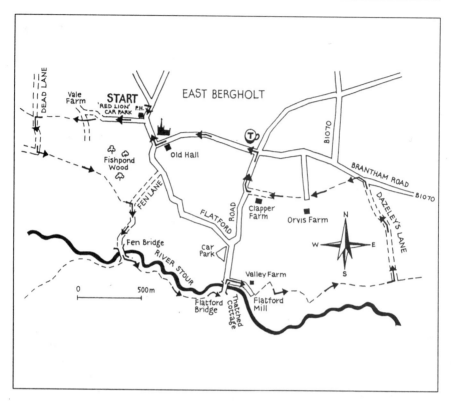

dry dock on the right behind the first gateway and featured in a Constable painting, and then past the Granary Barn. Pass through the gate at the end by the mill and along the drive to Willy Lott's Cottage, the site where Constable painted his most famous painting, The Haywain.

Bear left in the meadow, following the path around the field, ignoring the double gate at the first corner. Look out for a left turn marked with a footpath sign, leaving the National Trust trail which continues around the field. Walk down a dip through the trees to a stile and meadow on the other side of the hedge.

Walk along the right edge of this field, past a pylon to reach a stile in the corner. Turn left along the left hedge through a series of gates and stiles to a double stile at the end of the section. The other side of these stiles is a little muddy where the cattle have been standing, continue along the left edge to a wooden cattle pen and a gate and stile on the left leading to Dazeley's Lane.

Follow the lane up hill to the Brantham Road and turn left on the roadside footway for about 50 metres. Turn left at the side of No. 1 Clarence Villas, on a narrow path between fence and hedge, to emerge out to a field. Cross straight over on the well defined path to the next section of path, between fence and hedge, to Orvis Lane.

Cross the lane to a short section of grass leading out to a field edge path. Walk on to a stile in the corner leading to a pasture. Follow the left fence, to a gate and rough stile in the corner, to join the drive to Clapper Farm. Follow the path down to the road but note that the route of the public right of way leaves the drive and crosses the small strip of fenced pasture on the right.

Turn right up Flatford Lane taking care of the approaching traffic heading for Flatford. Turn left at the cross-roads at Burnt Oak on the main street, The Haywain Tea Shop is on the right and the White Horse pub opposite. Follow the roadside footway down hill and up to the church. Enter the churchyard via the rear gate and bear right past the unique bell cage to the main entrance. Follow the roadside footway on the right to return to the Red Lion pub and the start of the walk at the public car park at the rear.

```
┌─────────────────────────────────────────────────────────┐
│                                                          │
│                  Walk 9: Eye                             │
│                                                          │
└─────────────────────────────────────────────────────────┘
```

Route: Town Moor – Moor Hall – Braiseworth – Old St Mary's Church – River Dove – Park Lane – Kings Bridge – Eye Town – Town Moor.

Terrain: Road, track and drive, pasture, field edge and cross field paths, 12 stiles, quite muddy.

Start: Town Moor (Playing Field), Eye, Ordnance Survey map reference TM 143736.

Length: 5 miles (two short cuts).

Map: Ordnance Survey Pathfinder sheet 964 Diss (South) and Botesdale (Explorer sheet 230B).

Public Transport: For details telephone Suffolk County Council's Public Transport Information Travel Line – 0645 583358.

Road Route: From A140, turn off east on B1117, turn right into Community Centre car park before entering town. Parking available at Town Moor/ Community Centre, Cross Street and Buckshorn Lane car parks.

Tea Shop

The Dove House Restaurant, 7 Lambseth Street, Eye IP23 7AG. Telephone 01379 870736. Proprietors Jean and Vic Cocks. Morning coffee and afternoon teas, cream teas, lunches, traditional Sunday roast choice of four meats. Seating for 45. Evening bookings taken for parties of 8 or more. Bed and Breakfast.

Open every day 10am to 5.30pm. Front door of oak is reputed to be 400 years old and from the Eye Town Hall.

The Town

The old town of Eye is tucked away in the countryside away from the heavy traffic of the A140, leaving it a tranquil place with a village atmosphere and a peaceful rural character. The name Eye comes from an old Saxon word for an island and, on examination, the town can be seen to be on a rise above the surrounding land.

This area was once all water and marshland and even now the

The Dove House Restaurant, Eye

River Dove overflows after very heavy rain and the low land becomes flooded. This is dominated by the castle mound, dating from Norman times with a 19th century folly ruin, it once also sported a windmill.

Until 1974 and local government reorganisation, Eye was the smallest borough in the country, today the status of a town is retained together with its mayor.

In the 1800s Eye was an important market town served with a railway and a population of over 2500. The local crafts and trades included brewing, flaxworks, footwear, lace and corsetry and of course agriculture.

The Walk

From the Community Centre and playing field car park, walk along the right edge of the Town Moor playing field until you reach a bridge into the adjoining plantation. This is the Town Moors Storm Memorial, an area re-planted after the great storm of 1987 which devastated this former poplar plantation. The re-planting has created a new landscape and the various patterns and arrangements of the new trees are well worth exploring.

Turn left after the bridge and follow the path to leave the end of the plantation via a concrete bridge, leading out to a track known as Moorhall Causeway. Turn right and just before Moor Hall, bear left over a stile at a gateway into a meadow. Keeping to the right edge, look out for a stile on the left where the meadow narrows. This is the first of two short cuts and links up with the return part of the walk along Park Lane.

Continue along the right edge of the pasture, signed as the Mid Suffolk Footpath, through two gate and stile combinations, to the red brick remains of Black Barn at the end. Cross the stile at the corner, leading to a section of field edge, and then a cross field path, heading for the left edge of Moor Hall Plantation ahead.

At the other side of the field cross a stile into another section of pasture, following the right hand boundary hedge. At the end of the hedge turn right through a gate and stile combination and then bear left across a small pasture to a stile in the hedge opposite. This leads out to an old green lane and for a second opportunity to short cut turn left.

For the main walk turn right, passing a gate on the right which may be across the lane to control the cattle. The lane gets very muddy here, but follow it all the way out to the road. Turn left into Braiseworth, passing the Old Rectory, The Orchards and at a road junction, the redundant church of New St Mary, which was built in 1857 and is being restored. Later in the walk we will pass the remains of Old St Mary church.

Turn left just past the former church, into the orchard via a ladder stile over the rabbit fencing. Follow the fence on the left through the orchards, bearing right at the gate of a reservoir, following the fence below the retaining embankment to reach a second ladder stile on the left over the rabbit fencing. This leads out to the green lane mentioned above where the second short cut rejoins the walk.

Turn right to reach the road at Old Church Farm. Turn left towards the farm house, following the Mid Suffolk Footpath signposts, taking the left fork through the farm buildings. On the right of the track at the rear of the farm is the ruin of Old St Mary Church, set in its churchyard complete with gravestones. A church was recorded here in 1086.

At the end of the track, continue on down the path between

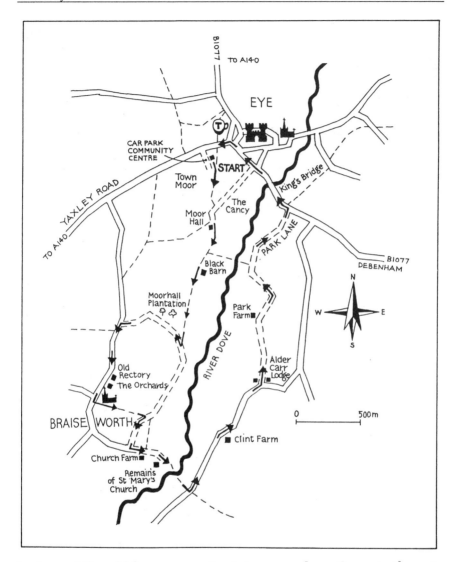

hedges of the old lane, emerging into a meadow. Cross to the gate and bridge over the River Dove, then across the end of an arable field to a gap in the hedge and a wide green section opposite. This leads to a field edge path with the hedge on the right and out to the road.

Turn left along the road, passing Clint Farm, and on as far as the first house on the left, Alder Carr Lodge. Turn left between the two lodge cottages on Park Lane, following the concrete track through Park Farm, around a pond, and on the other side where the lane changes to a grass track. Pass through a gate and stile combination and follow the track towards Eye. Ignore a joining track on the left, and after awhile, note the path joining from the left which is where the first short cut rejoins the walk.

Follow Park Lane out to the road and turn left on the roadside footway, crossing the River Dove and up into Eye. At the Midland Bank turn left on Magdalen Street and then left opposite Grampian Foods, on the public footpath leading to the playing field. Follow the path around the Community Centre to return to the start of the walk at the car park.

Walk 10: Felixstowe Ferry

Route: Ferry car park – Felixstowe Marshes – Kings Fleet – Deben Lodge Farm – Lower Falkenham – Sheepgate Lane – Falkenham Marshes – River Deben – Ferry Café car park.

Terrain: River wall, track, road and field edge, 5 stiles.

Start: Felixstowe Ferry, Ordnance Survey map reference TM 328376.

Length: 6 miles (no short cuts).

Map: Ordnance Survey Pathfinder sheet 1054 Felixstowe and Harwich (Explorer sheet 197).

Public Transport: For details telephone Suffolk County Council's Public Transport Information TraveLine – 0645 583358.

Road Route: From Ipswich on A14 to Felixstowe then follow signs for North Felixstowe and Sailing and Water Ski Club.

The Tea Shop

Ferry Café, Felixstowe Ferry, Felixstowe IP19 9BJ. Telephone 01394 276305. Proprietor Mrs Laura Balsom. Sandwiches and rolls, cakes (mainly home made), tea, coffee, cold drinks, ice cream, sweets and newspapers. All day breakfast, full menu for the whole day, salads, omelettes. Speciality local freshly caught fish.

Open 7 days a week, Monday to Friday 8am to 4pm, Saturday and Sunday 7am to 5pm, (later closing during the summer months). Seating for 50.

Martello Towers

The round Martello Towers were built between 1809 and 1812 as a defence against possible invasion by Napoleon, their walls are up to $4\frac{1}{2}$ metres thick to withstand incoming cannonballs. The guns were positioned on the roof to repel the invading enemy. Some 29 were built on the East Anglian coast between St Osyth in Essex in the south and Aldeburgh to the north, only 17 remain, either derelict or converted to houses.

The towers at Felixstowe Ferry are the T and V Martello Towers

Ferry Cafe, Felixstowe Ferry

and are clearly visible along the coastline. The V tower close to the Ferry was a coastguard lookout for many years but is now in private ownership.

Kings Fleet

This low lying area adjoining the River Deben was once part of the former harbour, known as Gosford Haven. Although now long since silted up, during the middle ages before about 1500, the haven extended through creeks and marshes, as far as Hemley. Kings Fleet was once connected to the river and is the long section of water between the Felixstowe and Falkenham Marshes. It was known as Kings Fleet because it sheltered warships of the medieval kings. Local history has it that Edward III assembled his expeditionary fleet in this harbour in 1346 before it sailed against Calais.

The Walk

From the car park at the side of the Ferry Café, take the tarmac path at the rear which starts from the roadside. This path is along the river wall, along the rear of boats of all shapes, sizes and conditions, settling on the mud banks of the River Deben. At the end of the tarmac section, turn right over a stile, to continue along the top of the river wall, now a little muddy underfoot when wet. Follow the river wall path on to another stile and shortly after, a junction of paths marked with a three arm footpath sign.

Turn left down the bank to a stony track with a gate and stile, walking to the right and parallel to Kings Fleet. Follow the lane alongside the water and continuing on as it turns away right and up to the higher ground at Deben Lodge Farm. After a barrier and low stile across the track at Deben Lodge, the public footpath becomes road. At the first junction with a signpost pointing towards Kirton, turn right towards Falkenham. Walk down through Lower Falkenham and up hill past Russels Farm on the left, as far as the next junction on the right.

If you wish to extend your walk to visit Falkenham Church turn left diagonally across the field towards the church which can be seen behind the trees on the other side. The church of St Ethelbert behind Falkenham Hall dates from the late 14th century and has a fine 15th century tower panelled in knapped flint and stone. Inside there is a handsome single hammer-beam and arch braced roof.

Turn right down Sheepgate Lane (marked Goseford Hall), and after 500 metres turn right at a footpath sign through a wide grass area. At the end continue on the edge of the field on the left on a wide grass track to the left of the ditch, look out for large numbers of swans which can often be seen in the fields ahead. At the corner of the field, turn left in the next field, following the edge with the drain on the left. Continue around the edge of the field to reach a footbridge and turn left after crossing. Follow this field edge round, again with the drain on the left, to reach a second footbridge. Turn left again and follow the field edge to reach the river wall at a path junction, marked with a three arm footpath sign.

On the top of the river wall look up river to the left where Ramsholt Quay can be seen in front of the distinctive pink Ramsholt Arms, the church with its round Saxon tower is just discernible in the trees on the hill.

Turn right and follow the bank top path alongside the river towards the sea on a wide grass track. There are fine views of Felixstowe Ferry and Bawdsey Manor on this stretch of the path. Bawdsey Manor was built by the Quilter family in the 1880s. It was

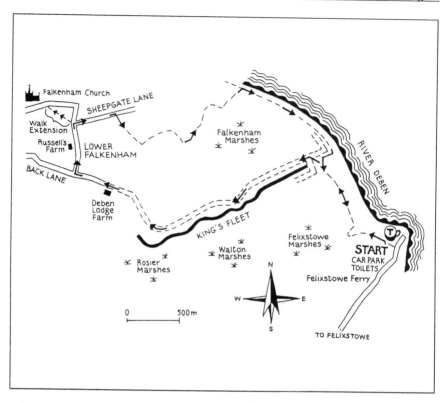

taken over by the Ministry of Defence in 1936 and it was here that Sir Robert Watson Watt developed radar. The distinctive mast can still be seen, the original masts were wooden and stood 240 feet high.

Continue along the river bank path, passing the jetties and jumping ramp used by the skiers of the East Suffolk Water Ski Club, and return to the three arm footpath sign marking the path junction at the end of Kings Fleet. Follow the path around to the left, retracing your steps over a stile to reach the second stile at the end of the tarmac path once again. Turn left along the surfaced path to return to the start of the walk at the Ferry Café and car park.

Walk 11: Framlingham

Route: Castle Inn – The Mere – New Road – White House Farm – Badingham Road – Saxmundham Road – Moat Farm – Coldhall Lane – New Barn – Edward's Farm – Brick Lane – Fairfield Crescent – The Knoll – Fore Street – Queens Head Alley – Market Hill – Castle Inn.

Terrain: Pasture, road, track and field edge, one stile, easy walking.

Start: Castle Inn, Church Street Ordnance Survey map reference TM 285635.

Length: 4½ miles (several short cuts).

Map: Ordnance Survey Pathfinder sheet 986 Framlingham and Saxmundham (Explorer sheet 212).

Public Transport: For details telephone Suffolk County Council's Public Transport Information TraveLine – 0645 583358.

Road Route: From A12 Wickham Market by-pass turn north on B1116, or from A1120 turn south on B1119, B1116 or B1120. Free car park off New Road.

The Tea Shop

The No. 10 Tea Shop, Market Hill, Framlingham IP13 9AN. Telephone 01728 621417. Proprietor Mrs Alison Mobbs. Tea, Earl Grey, herbal. Coffee by the cup or a cafetiere, hot chocolate, sodas, milk, squashes, sandwiches and baps. Home made cakes and fancies, daily selection of cakes, toasted tea-cakes, scones, cream teas, ice cream sundaes, soda floats. Light meals, ploughman's, salads, jacket potatoes, soup. Specials of the day are on the blackboard.

Opening hours Monday to Saturday 10am to 5pm also Easter to October Sunday 2pm to 5pm. Seating for 28, no dogs. The tea shop is in the central part of Framlingham and is part of a china shop.

Framlingham

Framlingham castle was built to last by Hugh Bigod in the 12th century and was one of the first castles to have a surrounding curtain wall and several towers, rather than a central keep. It is one of the

The Mere and Framlingham Castle

finest examples of curtain walled castle to be found, but of the original building, only the outer walls, towers and earthworks remain to dominate the surrounding countryside.

The monument is now cared for by English Heritage and is open April to September – daily from 10am to 6pm, October to March – daily from 10am to 4pm.

The castle was the seat of three powerful families, the Bigods, Mowbrays and Howards, from the time of the first Norman kings of England until the accession of Mary Tudor to the throne in 1553. After the death of Edward VI Princess Mary spent a long summer in the castle waiting to hear if she or Lady Jane Grey was to be declared Queen. Her Roman Catholic supporters camped outside to await the news, while her standard flew from the castle's towers.

Here also lived Thomas Howard, the first Duke of Norfolk, who won the Battle of Flodden for Henry VIII, when he died in 1524 he was buried at Thetford Priory.

Across the Mere and overlooking valley of the River Ore stands the impressive red brick Framlingham College. A Victorian built public school erected in memory of Prince Albert, it is said, with money left over from the building of the Albert Memorial in London.

The parish church of St Michael's has a tower standing nearly 30 metres high. Inside are painted alabaster tombs of the Howards with effigies of the Earl of Surrey, who was beheaded by Henry VIII on a trumped-up charge of treason, and his father.

The Walk

From the white gate adjacent to the Castle Inn, take the path down towards the Mere, from here there is a fine view of the Castle and the earth ramparts. At the bottom of the hill, pass through a gate and turn right, following the circular walk way marks. The Mere was dug out in about 1190 on the instructions of Roger Bigod II. Here the walk enters a Suffolk Wildlife Trust Nature Reserve where a wide variety of plants and birds can be seen. Follow the path through a series of gates and small bridges to reach the River Ore. Cross the footbridge to the playing field and turn right along the river bank to reach another footbridge and then out to New Road by the road bridge.

Turn right along New Road and after 500 metres follow the road round to the right past the entrance to Gt. Lodge Farms and then uphill. After a further 200 metres, a circular walk can be used as a short cut right if required. This area was formerly covered by Old Frith's Wood, once a hunting forest used by the owners of the Castle. Continue straight on along the road and just before White House Farm turn right over a stile and footbridge into the field.

Follow the path on the left edge of the field to reach the Badingham Road via a narrow footbridge. Turn left and at the left bend, turn right by an ash tree on a field edge path and crop break strip to the far side. Cross another small footbridge into the next field and turn right along the field edge, walking around the boundary of the field with the ditch on the right.

The path eventually reaches a grass track to the left which, if followed, zigzags in the general direction of the white water tower ahead and will bring you out at Moat Farm on the Saxmundham Road. Cross over to the farm drive but bear immediately right, around the side of the farm house and buildings on a field edge path. At the rear of the farm continue straight on along the left of the hedge, on a wide grass path, to reach Coldhall Lane.

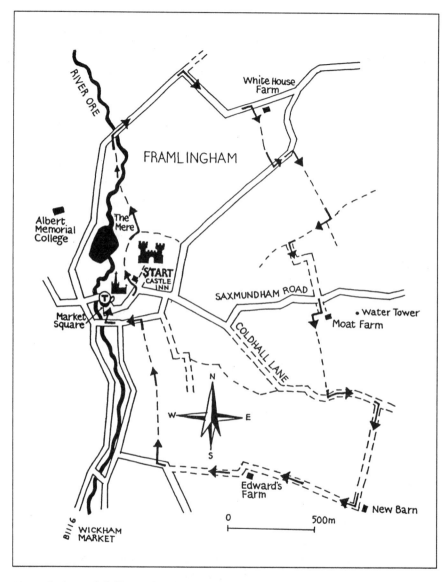

Turn left and follow the lane to a barrier and then right along the
track to New Barn. On fine days, splendid views of the surrounding
countryside and arable farming practice can be seen from this area.
Turn right at New Barn on the track heading for Edward's Farm,
which is on the rise ahead. Just before passing through the farm, turn

right, following the path around the side of the buildings to return to the farm drive on the other side of the farm. Turn right and walk on to reach Brick Lane.

Turn right on the road for 75 metres and then right again on the footpath across the fields. Continue along the rear of the houses ahead and eventually down some steps to Fairfield Crescent. Walk to the bottom of the hill and then right to the footbridge on the left, leading to The Knoll. Walk straight on up the side of the Cemetery, the old part of which is managed to encourage wildflowers and birds, to reach Fore Street.

Turn left along the roadside footway down to Queens Head Alley on the right, marked with white railing on the corner. Follow the brick path up through a splendid alley way in the half timbered building to emerge onto Market Hill. Follow the footway on the right, along Church Street to return to the start of the walk at the Castle Inn.

Walk 12: Hadleigh

Route: Magdalen Road – George Street – Tower Mill Lane – Durrants Farm – Valley Farm Lane – Valley Farm – Pond Hall Road – The Great Embankment – Hadleigh Railway Walk – Cranworth Road – Benton Street – River Brett – Layham Road – Tinkers Lane – Toppesfield Bridge – Riverside Walk – Corks Lane – High Street – Angel Street – Magdalen Road.

Terrain: Road, track, field edge, pasture and former railway track bed, 7 stiles.

Start: Magdalen Street car park Ordnance Survey map reference TM 027426.

Length: 6 miles (several short cuts).

Map: Ordnance Survey Pathfinder sheet 1030 Ipswich and Hadleigh (Explorer sheet 196).

Public Transport: For details telephone Suffolk County Council's Public Transport Information TraveLine – 0645 583358.

Road Route: From Ipswich or Sudbury on A1071, from Bury St. Edmunds A1141 to Hadleigh town centre, the entrance to the free car park is off Magdalen Road, parallel to High Street.

Tea Shop

The Spinning Wheel Restaurant, 117 – 119 High Street, Hadleigh IP7 5EJ. Telephone 01473 822175. Proprietor Mr Fazzoni. Pots of tea, coffee in cafetiere, decaffeinated, cappuccino, expresso, home made short bread, toasted tea cakes, scone, jam and cream, gateaux. Lunches, starters, soup, fish, chicken, duck, lamb, steak, risotto's, scampi tails, Torbay sole, liver and bacon, fresh vegetables and mixed salad.

Opening hours Monday to Saturday 9am to 2pm and 7pm to 9pm, Sunday 9am to 4pm. Seating for 70. Licenced, smoking and non-smoking areas. Member of the British Restaurants and Hotels Association.

15th Century Chapel, Hadleigh

Hadleigh

Around the fine church are grouped many lovely buildings, including the Deanery Tower, and beautiful specimens of Tudor architecture, including the timbered Guildhall. A prominent memorial erected on Aldham Common records the death of a famous citizen of Hadleigh, Dr Rowland Taylor. As rector of Hadleigh he was burnt at the stake for refusing Mass to be celebrated in the church during the reign of Queen Mary. The memorial, situated close to the junction of Lady Lane and the new by-pass, marks the spot where this macabre act took place. An inscription in the stone records the date of 1555.

On the walk you will pass the Toppesfield Bridge on Duke Street. This lovely old bridge spans the River Brett and although it is said to be of 14th century construction, it still bears today's traffic quite ably. Not only is it a Class II listed building, it is also a Scheduled Ancient Monument. Constructed mainly in red brick and stone with three arches, there is a parapet on each side finished at each end with an octagonal brick pier and ball finial.

The Hadleigh Railway Walk is a permissive path on the track bed of the former Bentley to Hadleigh branch line. Opened in 1847 the line served Hadleigh and intermediate stations at Raydon and Capel St Mary until it finally closed in 1965. Originally intended to continue on to connect with the Long Melford to Bury line, it was never completed and Hadleigh remained the terminus. The walk is open as far as Raydon and with the stations and bridges still intact, all that is required are the rails and a train to bring the line back to life.

The Walk

From the Magdalen Road car park turn left and left again into George Street, noting the many half timbered houses and, higher up the street, a 15th century chapel in front of the almshouses. Continue to the top of the road and on to Tower Mill Lane, following the farm track to Durrant's Farm. Fork left just before the house and keeping close to the hedge on the left, walk through the garden into the field beyond. Continue on the wide field edge with a ditch to the left to the end of the field and pass through a gap in the next hedge. Follow a good headland path around the left of the next field, crossing two sleeper bridges to join a grass bridleway.

Turn right to the farm yard, turning right and then left to join the tarmac drive past Valley Farm house. Continue along Valley Farm Lane to join Pond Hall Road near an engineering works. Turn left along the road and down around some bends, taking extreme care of the fast moving traffic and using the verge wherever possible.

Opposite the entrance to Pond Hall Farm turn right at the side of a galvanised gate, onto a green lane. Walk under a pylon and over two stiles through two pleasant meadows to a stile alongside a large tree at the foot of the railway embankment. The last few yards are always a little marshy, cross the stile and bridge over a stream and follow a well worn path through the trees to some old steps leading up the Great Embankment. The 50 foot high embankment was once the highest railway embankment in Suffolk and it is recorded that the first sod was ceremoniously cut on 5th September 1846, followed by a dinner for 40 gentlemen in a tent nearby.

The public right of way continues in the field to the right, parallel to the embankment but if you have the energy you can climb the steep bank to enjoy some extensive views south west towards Layham. Turn right and follow the old track bed towards the town for about a mile, after crossing the red brick Hooks Lane Bridge, look out for some steps down to Cranworth Road on the left.

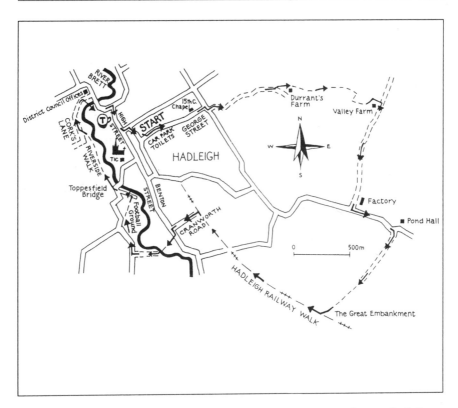

Follow the road side footway out to Benton Street and turn left for a short distance and cross to a stile at the end of the brick wall guarding the entrance to a footpath across a section of pasture. Follow the path through three sections of meadow and across the cart bridge over the River Brett. Continue on to a gate and stile along the farm track. The recorded route of the path soon leaves the track to follow the river bank in the field on the right but is difficult because of the fences. Therefore, follow the concrete track out to the Layham Road and turn right, after the bends turn right onto the playing fields.

Follow the roadside hedge to the car park and cross to the footpath at the rear of the pavilion. Follow this first between chain link fences and then right between hedges and out onto Tinkers Lane, close to the site of the former Hadleigh Mill. Turn left along Tinkers Lane at the side of the River Brett to Toppesfield Bridge and cross to the start of the Riverside Walk. This path has been improved by Babergh District Council to enable mothers with prams, wheelchair users and people who want an easy walk the opportunity to stroll by the river. On hot summer days this is an ideal place to find some cool shade, watch the wild life on the water or just get away from the hustle and bustle of everyday life. There are even picnic tables to sit at if you feel like a rest.

Follow the riverside path to the end where it emerges onto Corks Lane. Turn right and, at the grass opposite the Babergh District Council Offices, turn right on the foot bridge over the River Brett. Follow the walkway out to Bridge Street and turn right on the roadside footway to the junction with the High Street. Turn right towards the centre of Hadleigh, passing the Spinning Wheel Restaurant, and then left on Angel Street and right on Magdalen Street to return to the start of the walk.

Walk 13: Holbrook

Route: The Street – Ipswich Road – Holbrook Church – Holbrook Mill – Holbrook Creek – River Stour – Stutton Church – Alton Reservoir – Brook Farm – Reade Road – The Street.

Terrain: Tarmac footpath, road, cross field and field edge path, pasture and river wall, 7 stiles.

Start: The Village Hall on The Street, Holbrook, Ordnance Survey map reference TM 168366.

Length: 6 miles (several short cuts).

Map: Ordnance Survey Pathfinder sheet 1053 Manningtree and Dedham (Explorer sheet 197).

Public Transport: For details telephone Suffolk County Council's Public Transport Information TraveLine – 0645 583358.

Road Route: From Ipswich Wherstead Road and The Strand under Orwell Bridge. At the top of Freston Hill turn off right on B 1080 to Holbrook. Turn right at the Tea Shop into The Street. On street parking.

The Tea Shop

The Tea Shop, Ipswich Road, Holbrook IP9 2QR. Telephone 01473 327746. Proprietor – Alison Dineen. Home made cakes and scones, a wide range of speciality teas and coffees, soft drinks. Lunch – baked potatoes, quiche and soup. Orders made up to take away including birthday cakes. Summer seating in the garden.

Opening hours – daily 10am to 6pm, Tuesday open from 9am, closed all day Monday.

Craft shop – turned bowls, paintings, bead earrings and soft goods.

Alternative tea shop – Lakeside Tea Room, Alton Reservoir Visitor Centre. Open daily during summer and weekends during winter.

Holbrook

Holbrook (hollow brook – meaning brook in a ravine) is situated in the centre of the Shotley Peninsula and has several worthy attrib-

The Tea Shop, Holbrook

utes to be seen on the walk. Holbrook Creek on the River Stour is within the Suffolk Coast and Heaths Area of Outstanding Natural Beauty and provides a safe haven for large numbers of over wintering birds and an anchorage for small boats. There is an uninterrupted view of Essex across the river, which is over a mile wide at this point, and evidence of former commercial use can be seen from the remains of old wooden barge wharves.

Royal Hospital School

The school was founded at Greenwich in 1694 for the sons of officers and men of the Royal Navy and Royal Marines. In 1935 the school moved from Greenwich to Holbrook after Mr Gifford Sherman Reade (1846 – 1929) had donated the site from his estate in appreciation for the work done by the Royal Navy in World War 1. The school is built on a site overlooking Holbrook Bay and is dominated by a clock tower 61-metres high.

Alton Water

The reservoir was constructed between June 1974 and December 1976 and was officially opened by the Princess Royal in 1987. It has a capacity of 200 million gallons and provides drinking water for the whole of Ipswich and the south-east corner of Suffolk. It covers an area of 158 hectares and is used for fishing, sailing and other water sports. There is a footpath, a cycle way, a number of car parks, nature reserves and picnic sites around the edges of this man made lake.

The Walk

From the village hall turn right, walking towards the primary school and then right through a staggered barrier on a tarmac path along the school fence. At the first path junction turn right and continue out to the Ipswich Road, through an old fashioned metal kissing gate.

Turn right along the road and cross to the drive leading to Arnold's Butchers, follow the drive and then a short section of path between a garage and electricity pole, out to a field. Walk diagonally right across the field to the corner, through the gap in the hedge and over the crossing track. Follow the path ahead on the left of the hedge with former park land and large oak trees on the left. Follow the path down into the bushes and trees, keeping to the right, onto a section of boardwalk made of railway sleepers and then up again to a gate and stile at the road.

Turn right for a short distance and then left over a stile, giving access to a small paddock. Cross the grass diagonally right to a second stile and gate and on in the second paddock to a stile at the red brick church yard wall. Turn left between fence and wall and then along a field edge down to the road. Turn right to the junction with the B1080 road. Cross left to the wooden boardwalk by the mill pond, passing Holbrook Mill, and on to the end of the walk way.

Turn left at the end and take the Mill Stream Path to the river, marked with a green footpath sign. Keep on this path all the way to Holbrook Creek. Turn right along the track at the rear of the Sailing Club and then up onto the river wall path. Keep on this path until the river wall turns inland. Look out for a set of steps down to the right and a small footbridge in a gap in the trees. Follow this field edge path to a left turn into a pretty hedge-lined path leading to Markwell's Farm. Continue straight past the farm and onto a cross field

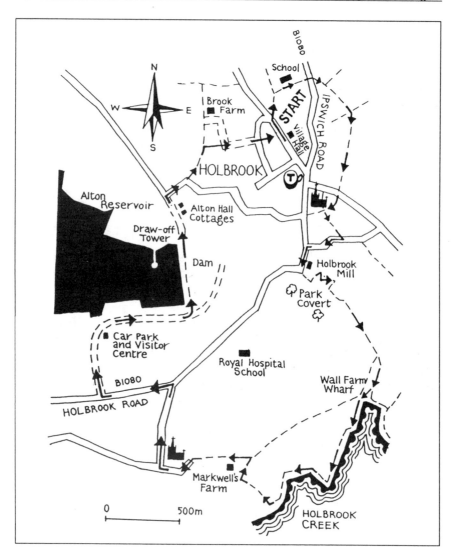

path to the far hedge. Turn left along the hedge to reach Stutton Church.

Walk up the road and turn right at the first junction by a barn. Follow the road to the main Holbrook Road, turn left on the footway to the entrance to Alton Reservoir. Turn right down the access road, to the Visitor Centre, Lakeside Tea Room and car park.

Continue along the road and then left across the dam to a white bridge over the reservoir overflow on the far side. Walk straight on across the grass to a gate and stile giving access to a stony track, passing Alton Hall Cottages, to reach the road.

Turn right along the road, to the first right bend and bear off left across the field, walking down to a footbridge at the side of a large tree. Continue on up the other side across a short cross field section and then along the hedge line. At the top turn right by a gap in the hedge, marked with a notice about keeping dogs on a lead.

Cross this field section down to the corner of the drive to Brook Farm that can be seen below and follow the track uphill between trees to Reade Road. Cross to a black metal kissing gate, designed to allow access for wheel chairs and prams, following the path between fences out to another metal kissing gate in The Street at the side of Holly Cottage. Turn right to return to the start of the walk at the Village Hall.

Walk 14: Ickworth

Route: Car park – Main Drive – Adkin's Wood – Lady Hervey's Wood – The Fairy Lake – The Canal – Canal Walk – White House – Old Coach Road – Mordaboy's Cottage – Ickworth Lodge – Tea Party Oak – Car park.

Terrain: Park tracks, woodland paths and drive, 4 stiles if the gates are locked.

Start: Ickworth Park car park and picnic area, Ordnance Survey map reference TL 815615.

Length: 4½ miles (several short cuts).

Map: Ordnance Survey Pathfinder sheet 984 Bury St Edmunds and Woolpit (Explorer sheet 211A).

Public Transport: For details telephone Suffolk County Council's Public Transport Information TraveLine – 0645 583358.

Road Route: From Ipswich A14 west or from Cambridge A14 east to Bury St Edmunds then follow brown tourist signs to Ickworth Park on the A 143 to Horringer village. Ickworth Park is 30 miles northwest of Ipswich and 3 miles southwest of Bury St Edmunds. Car Parking and entrance fee at Ickworth House is £2 per day.

Tea Shop

The Old Servants' Hall Restaurant, Ickworth House, The Rotunda, Horringer, Bury St. Edmunds IP29 5QE. Telephone 01284 735086. Proprietor The National Trust, Catering Manager Mary Berry. Pots and cups of tea, Yorkshire, Earl Grey or Darjeeling. Coffee, cup or cafitiere, Kenco and decaffeinated, hot chocolate, home-made orange and lemon squash.

Homemade cakes, sweet and savoury scones and various specialties each day.

Hot and cold lunches, soup, filled jacket potatoes, pies and casseroles and a vegetarian hot dish. Sweets. Children's portions and tuck boxes for children to carry their snacks. Lunches 12noon to 2pm and teas 2pm to 5pm. Table licence, no smoking.

Opening hours March to October 12pm to 5pm Tuesday, Wednes-

Ickworth House (and Tea Shop)

day, Friday, Saturday, Sunday and Bank Holiday Mondays November to March 11am to 4pm Saturday and Sunday. Admission with park ticket, seating for 60+.

Ickworth Park

Ickworth Park passed to the National Trust on the death of the 4th Marquis of Bristol in 1956, there are 729 hectares of formal park, woods and farmland. Most of the roads and tracks on the estate are now available for walking and recreation by the public. There are waymarked trails from two to eight miles long and with the many other paths crossing the park, provide a wide variety of walks in this historic parkland landscape. There are entrance fees for the park and gardens and for the house (National Trust members free). Telephone 01284 735270/735151 for information.

Whilst walking in the park, lookout for deer which can be seen through the trees or crossing open areas, and bunches of mistletoe growing naturally in the branches of the trees.

Opening hours – Park daily 7am to 7pm or dusk if earlier. House

1pm to 5pm, gardens 10am to 5pm March to November Tuesday, Wednesday, Friday, Saturday, Sunday and Bank Holidays. Shop 12noon to 5pm same days as house.

Information leaflets about the park with a map showing the various routes of the walks are available from a machine in car park priced £1.

The Walk

The walk described here is a combination of sections of the red and blue routes shown on the leaflet and way marked on the ground with coloured posts. From the main car park, return down the main drive past the ticket kiosk and, just before the main gate, turn right through a gate into the woods, following the red and blue waymark posts. At the first junction of the track turn right and after a short while note the stone on the right inscribed 'Adkins Wood planted 1800 – 1812'. Turn right at the next junction and then right again, following the path to the end of Fontainbleau Grove.

Turn right into the corner of the field where there is a good view of Ickworth House across the fields. Turn left into Lady Hervey's Wood, following the path parallel to the edge, to reach a crossing track. Turn left along the end of The Fairy Lake and then right at the other side down some steps at the side of the lake overflow. This is where the blue route leaves the red route, pass through a wooden barrier and through the woods to a footbridge leading to a grassy path along the side of the River Linnet.

At the first junction turn left to follow the path along the edge of the river and, just before the walled garden, turn left over a bridge and through a gate to continue along the Canal Walk. From here there are good views across The Canal, walled garden, summer house, private church and the Rotunda of Ickworth House at the rear. Continue along the left side of the Linnet down the valley, heading for the White House that can be seen in the trees ahead.

There are opportunities to short cut back to the start via the church by turning right across the canal on the paths and tracks of the blue route. At White House negotiate the fence and rejoin the red route and track ahead, still on the left of the river. When you reach the crossing embankment on the right, near the end of the track, you are on the dry bed of a former lake or reservoir, created in 1820 but

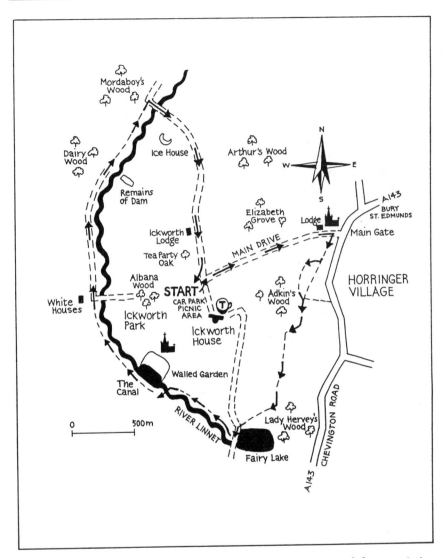

gone by 1885. The embankment is all that remains of the retaining dam built to hold the water in the lake.

At the next gate pass into the parkland pasture area, as you walk along the old coach road, look out for the mistletoe growing profusely in the trees. At the other end of the pasture at Mordaboy's Cottage pass through the gate and turn right up the access track into the upper park. Look out for the group of trees on the hill on the right where the old ice house is situated, the top of the underground building can just be seen in the trees.

After passing Ickworth Lodge, which was the Bristol family home from 1710 until 1828, there is a 700 year old pollarded oak tree on the right. The tree is known locally as the Tea Party Oak and is reckoned to be one of the oldest in England. This is where the children of Horringer School played games and had their treats for over 50 years from 1860. The tree is now fenced off and surgery is required to preserve and prevent it becoming dangerous.

Continue along the drive to return to the start of walk at the car park and picnic area.

Walk 15: Kedington

Route: Church Walk – West End Lane – River Stour – Calford Green – Haverhill – Mill Lane – Kedington Mill – Kedington Church.

Terrain: Track, road and field edge, no stiles.

Start: Kedington Church, Ordnance Survey map reference TL705470.

Length: 4 miles (two short cuts).

Map: Ordnance Survey Pathfinder sheet 1028 Haverhill and Clare (Explorer sheet 210).

Public Transport: For details telephone Suffolk County Council's Public Transport Information Travel Line – 0645 583358.

Road Route: From Bury St Edmunds on A143 turn off left before Haverhill. From Ipswich and Colchester via Long Melford turn right (north) off A1092 after Stoke by Clare.

The Tea Shop

Ketton Tea Rooms, Gardens and Antiques, West End Lane, Kedington. Telephone 01440 706770. Proprietor Ann Huxley. Specialises in gateaux, traditional cream teas winter and summer alike. Menu changes every day, gardens open during the summer and real log fire in tea room in winter. No lunches as such but a selection of sandwiches and toasted sandwiches. Home made crumpets, tea buns, preserves, ice cream and special ice cream sundaes. Group bookings and wheel chairs can be accommodated.

Open Monday, Tuesday, Thursday, Friday and Saturday 9.30am to 5.30pm, Sunday 2pm to 5.30pm, Wednesday closed, open on bank holidays.

Kedington

Kedington was formerly known as Ketton and since the 1960s has grown as part of the development of Haverhill. The church of St Peter and St Paul is known locally as the Cathedral of West Suffolk and sits prominently on a hill overlooking the River Stour valley. Risbridge Hospital was formerly the Union Workhouse, built in 1856 to

Cottage at Keddington

house 654 inmates. During the 1914-18 war it was used as a camp for conscientious objectors and prisoners of war. It reverted to a workhouse until 1937 when it was converted to a mental hospital.

The River Stour

A mill at Kedington was recorded in the Domesday Book, the present mill was rebuilt in the 18th century but ceased working in 1901. The River Stour enters Suffolk at Great Bradley and it is here that it receives a torrent of water from the pumping station at Kirtling Green, pumped up from the Little Ouse at Ely and the Cambridgeshire rivers and levels. The volume of water gives the river urgency and swiftly flows down through the Suffolk and Essex countryside to be pumped out again at Stratford St Mary in order to provide much need drinking water to the dry county of Essex.

The Stour Valley Footpath

The Stour Valley Path is a long distance walk stretching from near the source, to the estuary of the river, winding its way through Suffolk, Cambridgeshire, and Essex, some of the country's most pleasant lowland countryside. Starting at Newmarket the path covers sixty miles of countryside along the valley, renowned for its artistic connections. The 60 mile regional route was officially opened at Clare Castle Country Park in May 1994, the culmination of four years preparatory work by the Dedham Vale and Stour Valley Countryside Project. The route is all on public rights of way and fully way-marked with arrows bearing a unique artist's palette and dragon fly logo.

The Walk

From the church cross the road and walk down Church Walk past the primary school. The avenue of alternate chestnut and lime trees provides a fine route to the lower village and emerges out onto West End Lane.

Turn right to pass the Ketton Tea Rooms and Gardens, Ketton was the former name of Kedington and several references can be found to the old name including Ketton House. Continue on to the bridge over the River Stour. If the water is flowing swiftly you are witnessing the remarkable use made of the river to channel water to Essex. If the water is quiet of course, the pumps are not in operation.

On the other side of the bridge take the lane to the left of the Barnardiston Arms pub. Follow this on past the football field and, where the tarmac ends, continue on to join a field edge path. Opposite Cotton Hall and before a footbridge on the left, turn right up across the field on a well defined crop break strip. At the top of the hill and before the electricity pole, turn and look back over the valley for a wonderful view of the upper Stour valley.

Continue on to the other side of the field onto the access drive of Eastcott's Farm Cottage and on, past the farm, to the B1061 road at Calford Green. Cross straight over along the track to the left of the green and the left of a weeping willow tree. Where the track runs out at The Old Chapel, continue straight on along a wide grass strip, between the raised field and a hedge.

At the end of the grass bear right, following the ditch to the corner of the field. Cross the ditch via a twin railway sleeper bridge and turn left, down the field edge, following the ditch on the left. Follow the field edge around to the right at the bottom and, at the next corner, bear off left on the track through the trees.

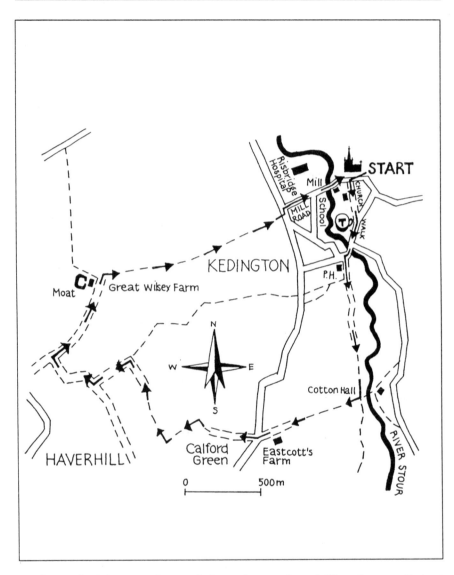

At the end of the wood, turn left on the track uphill to the tree line at the top marking the boundary of the outskirts of Haverhill. Pass through the trees and turn right along a stony crossing track. At the end of the trees turn right on the drive to Great Wisley Farm, following the track down and then up through the farm complex.

At the other side of the farm bear right on the clearly defined grassy field edge track, heading now straight towards Kedington. On the top of the rise Kedington Church will come into view ahead. At the end of the grass strip, continue across a twin railway sleeper bridge and then a crop break strip in the next field, downhill to the houses and out to the road by a telephone kiosk. Turn left and then right into Mill Road, walking on the roadside footway as far as School Road. Continue straight on along the road towards the river and to avoid some of the road traffic, turn right into the playing field, then walk along the left hedge to the river.

Return to the road and cross the river by Kedington Mill, continuing up the hill on the roadside footway to return to the start of the walk at the church.

Walk 16: Kessingland

Route: Church Road – Marsh Lane – Pedlar's Lane – Coopers Lane – Church Road – High Street – The Avenue – A12 by-pass – Marsh Farm – Pond Farm – London Road – Ashley Coffee Shop – Kessingland Cliffs – Green Lane – Promenade – Church Road.

Terrain: Mainly good tracks, field edge and a short cross field section, 4 stiles.

Start: Public car park, Church Road – Ordnance Survey map reference TM 533861.

Length: 4½ miles (several short cuts).

Map: Ordnance Survey Pathfinder sheet 946 Beccles(South) (Explorer sheet 231).

Public Transport: For details telephone Suffolk County Council's Public Transport Information Travel Line – 0645 583358.

Road Route: From A12 north or south, follow signs for the beach at roundabouts at either end of Kessingland by-pass to free car park on Church Lane.

Tea Shop

The Ashley Coffee Shop and Restaurant, Ashley Garden Centre, London Road, Kessingland NR33 7PL. Telephone 01502 740264. Proprietor Mr M Platt. Pots of tea, coffee, hot chocolate, milk, squash and cold drinks. Sandwiches and rolls, snacks including toast, toasted tea cakes, scones, selection of sliced cakes, cream teas. Hot lunches including lasagne, vegetable curry, vegetable sausage, with rice, baked potato or chips, beans and spaghetti on toast. Fish and chips, burgers. Various salads, selection of daily sweets on a black-board. Children's meals.

Open every day – Monday to Saturday 9.30am to 5.30pm (5pm winter) and Sunday 10.30am to 4.30pm.

Seating for 38, no smoking.

Coopers Lane, Kessingland

Kessingland

There has been a settlement at Kessingland since Palaeolithic times and between the Hundred River and Latimer Dam there was once a large estuary which was used by the Vikings and Romans. The sea provided the village with its main livelihood and at one time the village paid a rent of 22 000 live herrings to their Lords which at that time made it more important than Lowestoft. The village was once two separate communities, The Beach and The Street, and it was not until the 1960s that a large housing estate united the village into a single community.

The 29 metre tower of St Edmund's church has been a landmark for seafarers since Agincourt. The church was supported by the nuns of St Glare until the Dissolution of the Monasteries. Kessingland has been a holiday centre from far off days and Sir Henry Rider Haggard, a famous past resident, had his holiday home at a cliff top house he called the Grange from the 1880s to 1925. Rudyard Kipling stayed there frequently. The property was developed into Catchpole's Holiday Camp in the late 1920s and the Denes were begun just before the Second World War. The population of Kessingland is about 4000 but during the summer months this nearly doubles with the influx of holiday-makers.

The Walk

From the car park on Church Road take the footpath at the rear which commences on a private drive, and then a track which then continues between the rear of the houses and a field. Keep straight on along the track which is Marsh Lane, passing the sewage works on the right and the parish council's common land on the left.

The track eventually reaches the corner of a field, continue on up the right side on the wide grass track, with a good view of the church tower to the right. This is Pedlar's Lane, cross a track called New Road and on to a cross-roads of tracks where the lane becomes tarmac and is called Coopers Lane. Follow this lane out to the road, turn left and cross to walk along the roadside footway of Church Road opposite to reach High Street, the old route of the A12.

Cross straight over and walk along The Avenue and, just after Kessingland Working Men's Club, turn left along a track. At the entrance to The Bungalow on the right, continue straight on along the footpath between hedge and fence to reach a stile at the A12 bound-

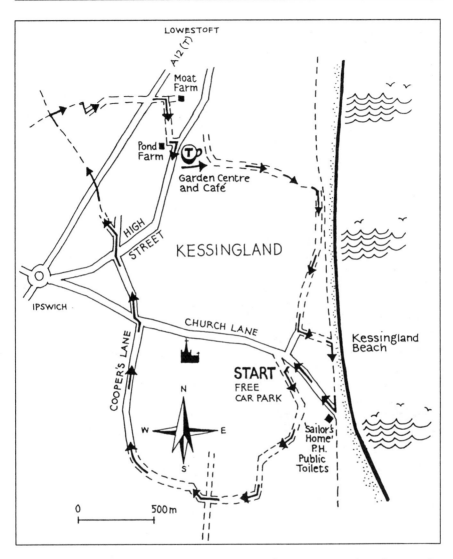

ary fence. Cross the dual carriageway with caution, using the gap in the crash barrier to reach a stile in the fence on the far side.

Cross the field ahead, the path should be well defined, and then in the next field on the path to the right of the hedge. At the top of the slope look out for a footpath sign where the path changes to the left side of the hedge and continues in the adjoining field with the hedge and ditch on the right. At an ash tree, cross the ditch on the right back to the other side, then look out for a crop break strip across the field ahead.

This grass strip turns to an open track by an electricity pole, and eventually between hedges to reach the A12 again at a stile. Cross again with caution, through the gap in the crash barrier, to a stile in the fence on the far side. Follow the concrete track ahead towards Moat Farm and, just before the farm buildings, turn right on a grass track towards Pond Farm. Turn left at the farm along the drive by the pond to reach London Road.

Turn right along the roadside footway past Ashley Garden Centre and Café and, just after the garden centre and a house, turn left through a gap in the hedge by an oak tree. This is a well worn permissive path along the field edge, turn left and then right at the end to join a track with trees and ditch on the left. At the end of the track continue on along the field edge path, with hedge and ditch on the left, to the end of the field and then up between the trees ahead. This is along part of the Suffolk Coast and Heaths Path, which runs for 50 miles between Lowestoft and Felixstowe.

On the cliff top turn right on the track, there are opportunities to turn left to the cliff and beach at various points along here if required. The track eventually becomes tarmac and, where the road turns right, continue straight on along Green Lane, a stony track, passing an information board about Kessingland and its path network. Follow Green Lane down hill, now on tarmac again, and look out for Coastguard Lane on the left, walk to the end and then down a set of steps to the beach.

Turn right along the promenade to the end of Church Road and then right, up past the Sailors Home pub, and on along the road to the car park and the start of the walk.

Walk 17: Lavenham

Route: Church Street – Water Street – Clay Hill Lane – Spraggs Wood – Hall Lane, Brent Eleigh – Cock Lane – Bear's Lane – Church Street.

Terrain: Road, track, wide field edges, no stiles, muddy in places after wet weather.

Start: Lavenham's Church Street car park, Ordnance Survey map reference TL 914489.

Length: 5 miles (no short cuts except by road).

Map: Ordnance Survey Pathfinder sheet 1029 Sudbury and Lavenham (Explorer sheet 196).

Public Transport: For details telephone Suffolk County Council's Public Transport Information Travel Line – 0645 583358.

Road Route: From Ipswich on A1071 to Hadleigh by-pass then A1141 to Lavenham centre. Lavenham is 15 miles west of Ipswich and 5 miles north east of Sudbury.

The Tea Shop

The Old Tea Shop, Church Street, Lavenham CO10 9SA. Telephone 01787 247248. Proprietor Mr Dawson. Morning coffee, light luncheons from 12noon to 2.30pm, afternoon teas, fresh scones daily, cake teas, crumpet teas, apple pie teas, sandwiches and snacks, scrambled eggs and bacon on toast, pots of tea, soft drinks, menu reviewed periodically.

Opening hours: Summer – Tuesday to Sunday 10.30am to 5.30pm, closed on Mondays. Winter – October to Easter, Saturday and Sunday 10.30am to 5.30pm, closed on weekdays.

Seating for 80. Former 15th century thatched glebe cottage until 1900, a tea shop since 1920.

Lavenham

There is much to see along the streets of Lavenham, half timbered houses stand at all angles and contrasting plaster colour washes abound in all directions. Lavenham was once the 14th wealthiest

Lavenham Church

town in England, the merchants of the cloth trade built their houses here and many of the magnificent buildings remain. A visit to the Tourist Information Centre in Lady Street will arm you with information and guides about the history and buildings of the town, there are also guided tours around the town if required.

The Market Place is well worth a visit and has remained virtually intact, with its market cross, medieval street pattern and the Guildhall, built in the 16th century, now used as a meeting place and museum. Lavenham's late 15th century church of St Peter and St Paul across the road from the tea shop is well worth a visit, the building measures 61 metres long and 21 metres wide with the tower standing 43 metres high. This gives the structure cathedral-like proportions and is reputed to be the highest church tower in England, a landmark that dominates the surrounding countryside from its hill top location and which can be seen for many miles around.

Other Walks in the area

Lavenham is one of those places on the tourist trail that attracts so many people that it can often detract from one's enjoyment of a visit. However there is a network of paths and lanes out in the countryside around the town, just waiting to be explored. There is a formal circular walk and a series of walks on the old railway lines promoted by the County Council for you try, as well as many other paths in the area.

Leaflets are available for the Lavenham Circular Walk, the Sudbury, Long Melford and Lavenham Railway Walks and a locally produced map of public rights of way from the Tourist Information Centre or Suffolk County Council if required.

The Walk

This is an alternative route from Lavenham to nearby Brent Eleigh, a picturesque village just off the main Lavenham to Hadleigh road and straddling the River Brett. A visit to the church in Brent Eleigh will reveal old box pews and wall murals for you to view, whilst at the local Cock Inn you will be provided with refreshment at the halfway point of your walk.

From Lavenham's Church Street car park, turn right on the roadside footway down to the Swan Inn and then right along Water Street.

Where the road bends sharply right and becomes Brent Eleigh Road, continue straight on along Water Lane past the Salvation Army Citadel on the left. After 150 metres turn right up Clay Lane, passing through Clayhill Farm where the lane becomes unsurfaced and can get quite muddy in places after wet weather. Follow the lane past Spragg's Wood on the left and on to reach Hall Road. Turn right and follow the road down to Brent Eleigh village, taking care of the fast approaching traffic, especially on the bends.

Follow the road down past the church, which is set back in the trees on the right, and over the old bridge across the River Brett to a road junction by an imposing red brick half timbered house. Bear right to the cross roads at the A1141 with the Cock Inn on the corner. Cross straight over and up Cock Lane, as you walk over the brow of the hill, turn back and look across the valley for a splendid view of the imposing Brent Eleigh Hall at the rear of the church. At the bottom of the dip cross a small bridge and turn right along a wide grass path to the left of the hedge, following the field edge to the end of the field and a crossing concrete track leading to Hill Farm.

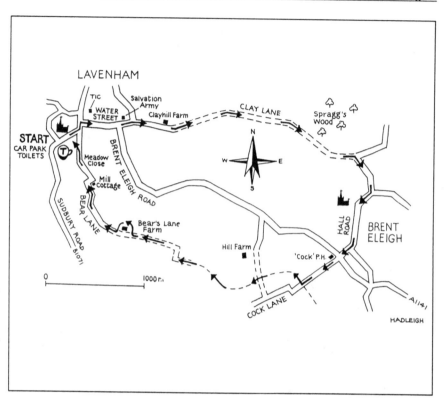

Turn right and immediately left, now on the right of the hedge, through a small section of plantation. Follow the path through a fine avenue of poplar trees to emerge on a wide field edge path to the left of a stream. Follow this to the end of the field and at a lone ash tree, continue straight on across a bridge into the next field, following the wide grass track to the left of the ditch. After about 150 metres follow the lane up to the right, now to the right of a hedge and turn left at the top on the track heading for Bear's Lane Farm.

At the gate to the farm turn sharply right, following the path around the edge of the farm complex on the field edge, and around the buildings until you meet Bear's Lane. Turn right towards Lavenham and follow the lane past Weaners Farm and Mill Cottage. When you have passed Meadow Close on the left, look out for a tarmac path at the next bend, this will lead out to Church Street and the start of the walk at the car park.

Walk 18: Long Melford

Route: Hall Street – The Green – Church of Holy Trinity – Kentwell Park – High Street – Hare Drift – Bypass – Roydon Drift – Bull Lane – Bypass – Melford Walk (former railway) – Station Road – Hall Street.

Terrain: Road and footway, field edge, pasture, track and former railway, 3 stiles.

Start: Long Melford main street, Ordnance Survey map reference TL 862455.

Length: 4½ miles (several short cuts).

Map: Ordnance Survey Pathfinder sheet 1029 Sudbury and Lavenham (Explorer sheet 196).

Public Transport: – For up to date travel information telephone the County Council's Public Transport Information TraveLine – 0645 583358.

Road Route: From Ipswich on A1071 to Sudbury, then A134 Sudbury bypass and B1064 to Long Melford. From Bury St Edmunds on A134 south. Plenty of parking areas on each side of the road.

Tea Shop

Antique Café, 1 Foundry House, Hall Street, Long Melford CO10 9JB. Telephone 01787 378535. Proprietor Tricia Stanley. Traditional dairy cream teas, home made cakes and bread pudding, apple pie, jam or treacle sponge and custard, sandwiches, kiddies corner, crisps and ice creams, jacket potatoes, soup of the day. Vegetarian choices, salads, omelettes, country ploughman's, scones, pot of tea, toasted tea cakes, early morning light bites, winter warmers and summer specials, disabled access. Adjoining the Hand Carved Candle Co, available for demonstrations, bookings for parties and events. Some tables for non smokers, seating for 35, licensed for beer and wine.

Opening Monday and Tuesday 10am to 5pm, Wednesday 10am to 5pm, Thursday, Friday and Saturday 10am to 5pm, Sunday 11am to 5pm.

Long Melford

Long Melford takes its name from the length of the main street and the Mill Ford which was once the crossing point of Chad Brook at the south end of the green. The village was once an important junction on the Roman road network and it is believed the straight main street is a remnant of one of the five roads that once converged here. Today the village is a popular centre for the antique trade, attracting a wide range of visitors.

The Green, Long Melford

The Railway

The 16 mile long Long Melford to Bury St Edmunds railway opened in 1865, with intermediate stations at Lavenham, Cockfield, Welnetham and Bury East Gate. The line was generally single track with double sections in places, in 1960 there were 5 trains a day using the line. Long Melford Station was at the south end of the village, close to the point where the railway walk ends at Station Road. The Melford to Lavenham section closed in 1961 and the Lavenham to Bury section in 1965. Several sections of the track bed are owned by Suffolk County Council and have been turned into a series of walks open to the public.

The Walk

The walk starts on the main street, called Hall Street and named to show its destination, the historic Melford and Kentwell Halls. Head north along Hall Street towards the church, there is a wealth of historic buildings including several pubs, hotels, restaurants and buildings converted into antique shops to see on the way. After crossing the Chad Brook follow the path to the left of the green, past the former school, aiming for the church ahead on the rise. There are many fine 15th and 18th century buildings to be seen around the green, built with wealth derived from the wool trade. Behind the wall on the right of the green, the roof of Melford Hall can be seen.

Cross the A1092 Clare Road with care and continue up to the church, passing the almshouses and hospital on either side of the road, built for the poor and destitute of the parish. The magnificent Holy Trinity Church was rebuilt in the late 15th century with donations from wealthy local families and has strong links with Kentwell Hall. In the churchyard bear left at the war memorial, following the drive towards the rectory, just before passing through the brick gateway note the old Long Melford station sign and lamp on the right, providing a link to the second section of this walk.

As the drive bears right, continue across a piece of grass to a pasture fence, following the path on the field edge for about 50 metres to a stile in the railings. Turn right and cross the small pasture to the corner and a stile to the right of the stable block. After a short section through the trees, cross another stile giving access out into the wide open pasture land of Kentwell Park.

Turn right along the south boundary, passing between a pond and the edge of the churchyard on the right, heading for a galvanised gate in the corner under the trees ahead. On reaching the drive to Kentwell Hall, glance to the left to see an avenue of trees leading to the Hall at the end. Can you see the mistletoe bunches high in the trees? Turn right to the main gate and then immediately left to cross the road to a concrete track, known as Hare Drift, to the left of a garden centre.

Follow the surfaced track through to the end at the new bypass and carefully cross to the gateway opposite. Turn right inside the field edge on a grassy track known as Roydon Drift, soon turning to the right and becoming a hedged lane down to the Chad Brook. Turn right on the bridge over the brook and then sharply left along the

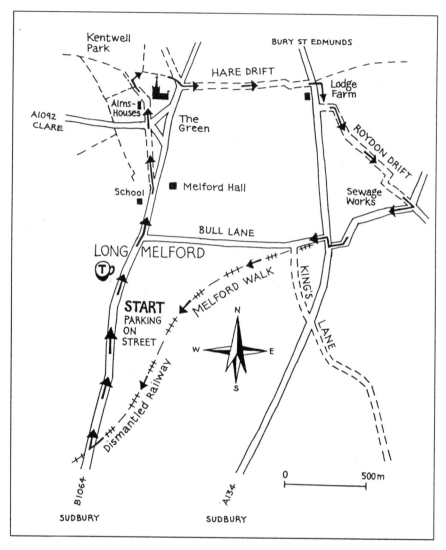

track, parallel to the brook on the other side. Walk past the sewage works and out to the road.

Turn right to the three way road junction and right again along Bull Lane, taking great care of the speeding traffic approaching over the hill, using the verge wherever possible. At Bull Lane Garage use the road side footway to reach the bypass once again. Cross with care to Bull Lane and just before the 30mph signs turn left and climb what is the remnants of the end of the embankment of the old railway line, now the Melford Railway Walk and maintained by Suffolk County Council.

By keeping to the route of the old track bed, cross Kings Lane, under two red brick bridges and eventually descend to Station Road, close to the point where Long Melford Station served the town. Turn right on the roadside footway and walk through the main street to your start point on Hall Street.

Walk 19: Mildenhall

Route: Kings Street – Mildenhall Museum – Market Street – Market Cross – St Mary's Church – Church Walk – Wamil Way – River Lark – Ely Road – Water Meadows – Barton Mills – Mildenhall Woods – River Lark – Jubilee Playing Fields.

Terrain: Surfaced and unmade paths, road and riverside, muddy in wet weather, no stiles.

Start: King Street car park, Mildenhall, Ordnance Survey map reference TL 711743.

Length: 4 miles (several short cuts).

Map: Ordnance Survey Pathfinder sheet 962 Mildenhall (Explorer sheet 229).

Public Transport: For details telephone Suffolk County Council's Public Transport Information Travel Line – 0645 583358.

Road Route: Mildenhall is 12 miles north west of Bury St Edmunds, 39 miles from Ipswich. From Bury St Edmunds, follow the B1106 and A1101 roads, signposted into Mildenhall. Turn left at the war memorial into King Street and the free car parks at the end of the street.

Tea Shop

Crusty Loaf Bakery and Lynn's Tea Rooms, 24 The Precinct, Mildenhall IP28 7EF. Telephone 01638 718989. Proprietors Mr and Mrs H Green. Teas, coffees, hot chocolate, soft drinks. Cakes, sandwiches, toasted sandwiches, jacket potatoes, chips, pasties, soup, salads. Bakery and full take away menu available. Seating for 32.

Open Monday to Saturday 7am to 5pm.

River Lark

The River Lark flows through the edge of the town and is often referred to as East Anglia's little known waterway. It was once navigable for 24 miles as far as Bury St Edmunds, providing an important trade route for the region and a link via the River Ouse to the sea at Kings Lynn. Sections of the river had been used for navigation from the Middle Ages but the first (unsuccessful) application to make the river navigable dates from around 1620. An Act of Parliament was eventually passed in 1699 allowing the river to be opened up as far as Bury St Edmunds. The work was completed by 1715 as far as Fornham, but was delayed from further progress until the Bury St Edmunds Borough Council had approved the scheme. Trade was at its highest between 1750 and 1850 but the opening of the railway on 2 June 1884 saw a rapid decline in the river traffic. The main trade was in coal going up the river with very little return cargo recorded on the way back. The public right of navigation still exists, although the derelict locks mean that progress can only be made by portage around the obstacles. Parts of the old tow path are now public right of way and the Lark Valley Footpath provides a 13 mile link for walkers between Mildenhall and Bury St Edmunds.

The Market Cross

RAF Mildenhall

The nearby airfield was the first of a series of new style bomber bases and opened on 16 October 1934. In the days before the Second World War the Royal Air Force played host to many peacetime events such as air races and Empire Day air shows. During the war the base became a bomber group headquarters, launching regular day and night bombing raids over Germany. Over 200 Mildenhall aircraft were lost and 1900 aircrew killed in action during this period. American bombers appeared at the base on 12 July 1950 in support of the US Nato commitment. Later, RAF Mildenhall became the gateway to the UK for all US military personnel arriving for service in Europe, with over 100 000 passengers passing through each year.

The Walk

From the King Street car park turn right to the Mildenhall Museum. Turn left along Market Street to the market square where the Market Cross and Parish Pump remind us of the rich history of the town. Turn left on High Street and then right on Church Walk, passing the mediaeval Church of St Mary. The buildings around the churchyard are worth a visit, old almshouses renovated by the Mildenhall Round Table, The Priory which was once the Parish Workhouse and other interesting cottages. Out on the High Street are former coaching inns with evidence of the arches, which allowed access to the stables at the rear.

Continue on along the walled section of Church Walk to Wamil Way. Turn left and, where the road bends to the right, continue straight on to the river through a staggered barrier leading to a path between fence and trees alongside the Mildenhall Cricket Pitch. At the water's edge you join the Lark Valley Path, turn left to cross a footbridge over the mill steam and along the path opposite the mill to Mill Bridge which carries the Ely Road.

Turn up left before going under the bridge, on reaching the road turn right and cross the river on the roadside footway. On the other side turn left on a track to return to the river side. The old locks in this area remind us of the river's golden age, more information and historic photographs are available in the museum. At the first footbridge over the river there is a short-cut back to the start if required. Follow the tow path past the end of the footbridge and then turn right away from the river, where the footpath leads across the water meadows conservation area, to Barton Mills.

When you emerge at the road continue straight on, keeping to the left verge where there is room to walk. Follow the road round and join the roadside footway at The Street, passing the mediaeval church of St Mary, the Bell public house and the village post office. Just after this point there is a plaque on the left side of the road inscribed 'This house was the country home of Sir Alexander Flemming FRS the discoverer of penicillin from 1921 to 1955'.

Continue on to the end of The Street and turn left on Old Mill Lane to the bridge over the River Lark, where further evidence of the old navigation can be found. At the end of the white railings turn left onto the former tow path, following the riverside walk through woodland and the edge of the playing fields back to Mildenhall. Along the gentle bends of the river many interesting plants and birds can be seen. In the summer months plants like the yellow flag iris growing in the shallow margins of the river and the purple loosestrife with purple flower spikes provide a splash of colour to the scene.

After passing the end of the footbridge over the upper level of the river, turn right up the fenced path towards the town centre and the start of the walk at the car park.

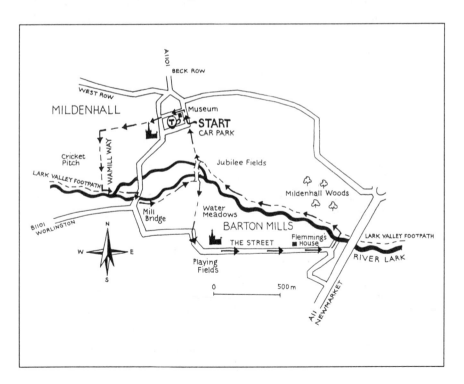

Walk 20: Needham Market

Route: Needham Lake – Alderson Lake – River Gipping – Darmsden – Darmsden Church – Barking Church – The Causeway – Hill House Farm – Stowmarket Road – Gypsy Lane – River Gipping – Alder Carr Farm – Needham Lake.

Terrain: Road, track field edge and riverside path, 8 stiles.

Start: Needham Lake visitor centre, Ordnance Survey map reference TM 094546.

Length: 7 miles (several short cuts).

Map: Ordnance Survey Pathfinder sheet 1007 Stowmarket and Coddenham (Explorer sheet 211B).

Public Transport: For details telephone Suffolk County Council's Public Transport Information TraveLine – 0645 583358. For rail travel information telephone 01473 693396.

Road Route: From the A14 follow the brown tourist information signs for Needham Lake, free car parking.

The Tea Shop

Alder Carr Farm Tea Room, Creeting St Mary Road, Needham Market IP6 8LX. Telephone 01449 721166. Proprietor Gillian Laws. Teas, Coffees and home made cakes.

Hot and cold light snacks, toasted sandwiches and baguettes a speciality. Seating for 20 with additional tables outside in the courtyard.

Opening Hours 10.30am to 5.30pm daily except closed on Mondays (open on Bank Holiday Mondays). Farm Shop, Pick your Own, Pottery, Woodworking, Garden Craft, Computer Training and Country Studio with resident artist. Alder Carr Farm lies beside the River Gipping, a short stroll from the old canal tow path used for part of the walk The old dairy buildings have been converted over the years, and now surround a pleasant courtyard where cows used to gather for milking. The tea room is situated in a former cow shed.

Needham Lake

This is an exhausted gravel extraction working turned into a popular water recreation area by Mid Suffolk District Council. A new car park has been built across the river, connected by a wide footbridge, to give access to the restored lock close to Bosmere Mill. The device in the centre of the lake is a wind operated water aerator, to keep the water fresh and algae free. The lake is used by model boat enthusiasts, who are often surrounded by the prolific waterfowl feeding from scraps provided by visitors.

Hawksmill, Needham Market

Darmsden

The little church at Darmsden stands out in the countryside away from roads and the bustle of every day life. A chapel existed here in 1460 but the present church was built in the Neo Gothic decorative style in 1880. The flint building was declared redundant in 1979.

Alder Carr Farm

This was once a dairy farm but is now a Farm Shop, Pick Your Own and countryside centre. There are a number of historical buildings including a mill built in 1796, originally at Creeting St Mary, brought down on an ox cart earlier this century. It has now been converted into a woodwork workshop. A traditional barn has been removed from near Bury St Edmunds and erected to provide more work shops. Previously called Houghton Park, Alder Carr Farm took its name from a nearby wood with an interesting history. It is thought that the Alder was planted to supply charcoal to the gunpowder factory at Stowmarket. The wood is now managed as a wildlife haven, with over 70 bird and 100 plant species recorded there.

The Walk

Start from the Needham Lake Visitor Centre and cross the river via the footbridge by the lake. Turn right on the Gipping Valley River Path, past the restored lock at Bosmere Mill, and out to the road. Cross to the entrance to the Alderson Lake area, following the river bank on the left. Cross a number of stiles and footbridges, past River-

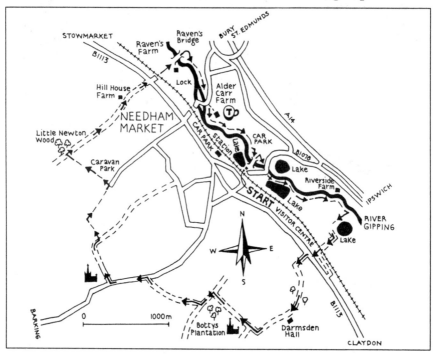

side Farm on the other bank. After the third footbridge turn right at the point marked with a footpath sign. This leads away from the river, past a lake, to a stony track at the rear.

Follow the track over a railway bridge and at the left bend, continue straight on along a wide field edge path to the road. Turn right for about 50 metres and then left on the private road to Darmsden, marked as a Public Footpath. Follow this road up through the farm complex and hamlet at Darmsden Hall.

Follow the signs to Darmsden Church then take the stony track to the right across the fields. At the top of the rise ahead, turn left on the track, passing the end of a conifer wood on the left called Bottys Plantation. There are some splendid views of the surrounding countryside from up here, the Ordnance Survey map shows the height to be 57 metres above sea level.

At the end of the plantation follow the track to the right, down hill all the way to the B1078 Barking Road. At the road turn left on the roadside footway for 400 metres and then right up the road, known as Parson's Lane towards Barking Church. Where the road turns sharply left, continue straight on along the bridleway, guarded by a white chain. Turn right and then left after a few yards to pick up the Causeway, an ancient tree lined lane leading back to Needham Market. The name Causeway is thought to be a corruption of 'corpseway', at one time Needham Market had no graveyard and burials were undertaken at Barking Church.

After a sharp right bend in the path, look out for a very large oak tree on the left, turn left here, through a gap in the hedge marked by a footpath sign. Walk along a well defined field edge path, over a footbridge to the corner, and then right on around the field to the opposite end. Take the track ahead, following it around to the left after a few metres, past the end of a caravan park to a stile at the corner by some conifer trees.

After crossing the stile, walk along the field edge path ahead, through two fields, to a concrete track at the edge of Little Newton Wood. Turn right along the concrete, following it down through Hill House Farm to emerge at the Stowmarket Road.

Cross carefully to Gipsy Lane opposite and follow this to the railway. Cross via the white pedestrian gates and remember to Stop, Look and Listen, especially to the right where the railway bends. Continue along the stony rack on the other side to Raven's Farm, bearing left of the wooden board fence to reach a stile and footbridge over the River Gipping.

Turn right along the Gipping Valley River Path, crossing two footbridges close to Hawks Mill, and on alongside the old lock, now used as a flood control gate, to reach the Creeting Road bridge. If you want to visit the Alder Carr Farm Shop and Tea Room, turn left along the road for a short distance and then right down the drive. Otherwise follow the path under the concrete road bridge to join a tarmac path leading to a black metal footbridge over the river.

Turn left over the stile to the field edge and on along the river path to the reach the main car park at Needham Lake. Turn right over the wooden footbridge leading to the alternative car park and the start of the walk at the Needham Lake Visitor Centre on the other side.

Walk 21: Orford

Route: Quay Street – River Ore – Doctor's Drift – Daphne Road – Bullockshed Lane – Ferry Road – Mill Broadway – Snape Road – Gedgrave Broom – Gedgrave Road – River Ore – Orford Quay – Quay Street.

Terrain: River wall path, field edge, track and road, 4 stiles.

Start: Quay Street car park, Orford, Ordnance Survey map reference TM 424496.

Length: 5 miles (several short cuts).

Map: Ordnance Survey Pathfinder sheet 1009 Aldeburgh and Orford (Explorer sheet 212).

Public Transport: For details telephone Suffolk County Council's Public Transport Information Travel Line – 0645 583358.

Road Route: From the A12 at Woodbridge by-pass take the A1152 and B1084 signposted to Orford. Pay and display car park at Quay Street, other on street parking in the town.

The Tea Shop

The Old Warehouse Restaurant, Quay Street, Orford IP12 2NN. Telephone 01394 450210. Proprietor Mr W Pinney. Morning coffees 10pm to 12noon and afternoon teas from 3pm.

Home made cakes and scones and snack menu. Lunches, starters, main courses and sweets. A board displays the day's special courses. The restaurant specialises in grilled or deep fried fish supplied from its own fishing boats landing their catches at Orford Quay.

Opening times – 10am to 6pm April to end October, closed Mondays except Bank Holidays. Open weekends throughout the winter. Seating for 50, licensed, no smoking, children welcome.

Orford

Orford lies on the banks of the River Ore and until the 16th century it was a bustling riverside port trading in fish and wool, during this prosperous era the original Norman Church was rebuilt. By the end of the 16th century the shingle spit of Orfordness had extended south, blocking the entrance to Orford Harbour. Trade decreased and the village went into decline, losing its Borough status in 1883.

The centre of the old town is well worth a visit with an old fashioned Market Square, Town Hall and many fine buildings. The connection with the sea is reflected in the construction of the houses, pubs and church, many of the timbers used are thought to originate from the shipbuilding industry and the sailing ships that took part in the Battle of Sole Bay in 1672.

The Rivers

The Rivers Ore and Alde were once separate rivers flowing into the sea at Orford and Aldeburgh, respectively. These two outflows have now both disappeared, with the result that the River Alde was deflected southward, running parallel and close to the coast-line, eventually joining the River Ore at Orford. The river is navigable up to the quay at Snape Maltings and Snape Bridge.

Orford Castle

The castle dominates the village and surrounding area and was commissioned by King Henry II in the 12th century as a fortified residence and coastal defence, it once marked the

Orford Castle

centre of medieval Orford. At this time the village extended to the south and west of the castle where there are fields today. The castle is a near perfect example of a Norman keep and is maintained by English Heritage. The walls are 3 metres thick and inside there is a maze of rooms and passages and even a two-seater loo. There is a spiral staircase to the top of the tower where there are fine panoramic views over Orford Ness and the sea.

Opening hours: 1 April – 30 September 10am – 6pm, 1 October – 31 March 10am – 4pm (closed 1 – 2pm). Telephone 01394 450472. Admission: adults £2.10, concessions £1.60, children £1.10 (under 5 free).

The Walk

From the Quay Street car park opposite the Jolly Sailor pub turn left towards the quay but turn left along the river wall path at the side of The Old Warehouse Restaurant. Follow the path past the front of Orford Sailing Club, across the water the red and white lighthouse and strange pagoda like buildings of the former Ministry of Defence Nuclear Research Station of Orfordness can be seen. The island has now been purchased by the National Trust and details of access are available on the quay.

After a stile the path continues along the open river wall, turn left at the next stile, down a set of steps and across a field to Doctors Drift, a grassy track once used for livestock access. Turn left along the track towards the village and out to Daphne Road. Turn right to reach Bullockshed Lane and then turn left to reach Ferry Road.

Cross straight over and continue along Mill Broadway to the main B1084 Snape Road. Cross this to a track opposite, following the edge of the trees and a row of electricity poles. (Look out for a short cut on the left for a route back to the village if required). Continue along the track to Gedgrave Broom where the track bears left down to the Gedgrave Road at Richmond Farm (look out for another short cut back to the castle on the left if required). Turn right along the road for about 350 metres and then left on a stony track heading down towards the river. Cross the stile at the end of the track and climb up the grassy slope onto the river wall.

Turn left along the river side path, around Chantry Point and on towards Orford Quay, passing through an unusual Rambler gate that can be parted to let you through, followed by a stile close by, To the left there is a good view of the castle which can be seen from most parts of this walk and dominates the flat river margins. Follow the river wall to a point close to the quay and bear right through a gap in the fence. Follow the path to the quay, taking time to explore the fishing boats and sailing craft and to smell the salt of the sea. Turn left up the road past the Warehouse Restaurant to return to the Jolly Sailor pub and the start of the walk at the car park opposite.

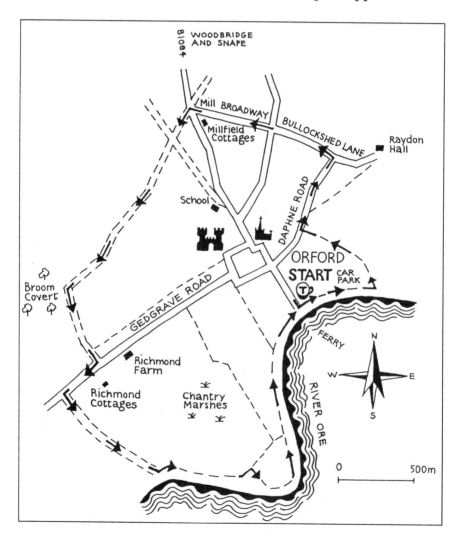

Walk 22: Peasenhall

Route: Village Centre – River Yox – Sibton White Horse – River Valley – Roman Road – Mill Road – School – Redham Road – Hencoop Wood – Abbey Farm – Village Centre.

Terrain: Pasture, field edge, tracks and road, no stiles, muddy in wet weather.

Start: Peasenhall Post Office, Ordnance Survey map reference TM 357694.

Length: 4 miles (several short cuts).

Map: Ordnance Survey Pathfinder sheets 965 Halesworth and 986 Framlingham and Saxmundham (Explorer sheet 231).

Public Transport: For details telephone Suffolk County Council's Public Transport Information TraveLine – 0645 583358.

Road Route: From Ipswich north on A12 to Saxmundham by-pass, then left following signs for Peasenhall. Alternatively along A1120 from either Yoxford or the A140.

Tea Shop

The Weavers Tea Rooms, The Knoll, Peasenhall IP17 2JE. Telephone 01728 660548. Proprietor Trudy Hollands. Traditional English tea, crumpets, toasted tea cakes, sandwiches. Cream teas with fresh scones, jam and cream plus freshly brewed tea. Full menu for lunches, dinners and suppers. Three course Sunday lunches and special menus for special events. Booking advisable. Senior citizens 3 course lunches on Tuesdays and Thursdays.

Open every day – Sunday to Friday 9am to 5.30pm, Saturday 9am to 9.30pm. Other evenings are by reservation. Seating for 45. The Weavers Pantry – Home made pickles, puddings, mincemeat, cakes, hampers and frozen food. Free delivery over £10.

Peasenhall and Sibton

A visit to the parishes of Peasenhall and Sibton is really a visit to only one village, physically they are joined with the east end of the main street in Sibton and the west end in Peasenhall. There has probably been a settlement here for 4000 years, the history of these integrated villages goes back a long way. Bronze Age implements have been found in Peasenhall and two major Roman roads met here to establish a settlement on either side of the river.

After the Norman Conquest the manor of Sibton was given to the Mallet family and Peasenhall to the Bigod family. The Mallet family founded the Abbey of the Blessed Virgin Mary which was the only Cistercian Abbey in Suffolk. The ruins can be seen across the valley from the A1120 road, near to Sibton Church.

One famous son of Peasenhall was James Josiah Smyth who, in the 19th century, invented and manufactured the Suffolk seed drill to be exported all over the world. The village sign is topped with a scale model of the drill with all its mechanical complications, as a memorial to this celebrated man.

The Walk

The walk is through both the parishes of Sibton and Peasenhall, and starts from the red telephone box near the Post Office in the main street. Turn right (east) and walk to the garage and turn left at the road junction, signed for Walpole and Halesworth. The village sign with the seed drill is on the right standing on The Knoll.

Follow the road left at the first junction, over the River Yox bridge and on along a roadside footway to the Sibton White Horse pub at the next junction. Turn left for about 100 metres and then left over a small footbridge into a section of pasture. Follow the river on the left, to the corner of the field, and over another footbridge to a grassy track.

Turn left for a few yards to cross the river and then right in a large section of pasture, following the bottom edge to an oak tree at the corner. Continue straight on along a crop break strip, with Valley Farm over to the right, to reach the road via another small footbridge. Turn left up the hill, this is an old Roman road, which connected with the Roman road from Coddenham (Combretorium) at the river crossing in the centre of Peasenhall.

After passing the brow of the hill, turn right at the first junction along Mill Road. On reaching the houses note the base of the old mill in the garden of the first house on the left. At the red telephone box, turn left down Mount Pleasant, following round to the left at the

The White Horse, Sibton

junction and then right by house No. 14, passing the front of the garages. Pass through a kissing gate in the left corner, across a meadow to another kissing gate opposite and then down the path past the school to the A1120 road.

Cross to the footway on the other side and walk left for a few metres to the path on the right, marked with a footpath sign by the white railings of a bridge. Follow the narrow path up along the left of a deep ditch, along a field edge and at the corner, down into the trees and along the ditch edge again, to reach the Bruiseyard Road, by a road bridge with white railings.

Turn left along the road for about 50 metres to a bend and turn right by an oak tree at Peasen House, up through a small gate and a narrow path between hedge and fence. Emerge through another small gate into a paddock and continue on up the left hedge to a gate at the corner.

Turn left along the field edge, walking on the left of the ditch to reach a track. Turn right and follow the track along the field edge until it turns left into the next field by an oak tree. Follow the path right, around the edges of the field, with the ditch on the right and lined at intervals with oak trees, to reach the Rendham Road.

Turn left, past a pink thatched cottage and a poultry complex and,

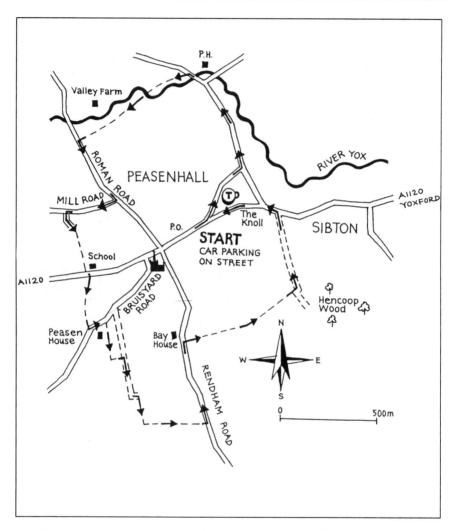

just before the road starts to slope down to the village at Bay House, turn right through a gateway on a wide field edge grass path. Keep to the left of the hedge and oak trees through three fields to the reach a track near Hencoop Wood. Turn left up the stony track, following it over the brow, to reach the A1120 road by the 30mph signs.

Turn left along the verge, noting the old school on the right which was founded in 1719, and continue on to join the footway along the river to return to the start of the walk in the main street.

Walk 23: Snape

Route: Snape Bridge – River Alde – Canser Path – Priory Road – Guilding's Lane – Church Road – Snape Common – Wadd Lane – Gromford Lane – Cundle Green – Abbey Farm – Snape Maltings.

Terrain: River wall, well used field paths, tracks and roadside footway, 1 stile.

Start: Snape Bridge, Ordnance Survey map reference TM 392576.

Length: 3½ miles.

Map: Ordnance Survey Pathfinder Series sheets 1008 Wickham Market and Area and 1009 Aldeburgh and Orford (Explorer sheet 212).

Public Transport: For details telephone Suffolk County Council's Public Transport Information TraveLine – 0645 583358.

Road Route: Turn off A12 on A1094 to Snape, which is 19 miles from Ipswich and 3 miles from Saxmundham. No public car park except for Maltings patrons.

The Tea Shop

The Granary Tea Shop, Snape Maltings, Saxmundham IP17 1SR. Telephone 01728 688303/5. Proprietor Snape Maltings Riverside Centre Partnership. Coffees including cappuccino, teas freshly brewed in the pot, hot chocolate, soft drinks and ice creams. Home made cakes baked on the premises, light snacks such as pies, quiche, rolls, soup and puddings.

Opening times – 10am to 5pm daily all year except Christmas Day and Boxing day.

Seating 30 – 40 with more tables outside in the summer, easy access for disabled and pushchairs, coaches by appointment.

For lunches and evening meals the adjoining Plough and Sail pub serves a menu of fresh, seasonal produce served in an informal atmosphere. Seating also available in the paved garden during the summer months. Bookings for evening meals telephone 01728 688413.

The Granary Tea Shop

Snape Maltings

The 19th century red brick maltings were formerly owned by Mr Newson Garrett who started the business in 1854, they became one of the largest maltings in the country. Barges took the malt out to breweries in London and Norwich and along the east coast and brought in cargoes such as coal to supply a coal merchant's business. In spite of a connection with the railway in 1859, the venture continued to operate commercially until 1965 when new techniques in the malting industry proved unsuitable for the old buildings.

The complex was bought by George Gooderham in 1965 and, situated only 5 miles from Aldeburgh, it was the ideal place for the Aldeburgh Festival Committee to convert into an opera house and concert hall. Although severely damaged by fire in 1969, rebuilding quickly took place, inspired by Benjamin Britten and Peter Pears. The concert hall is internationally renowned for its fine acoustics and together with the Britten/Pears school for Advanced Musical Studies, attracts visitors from all over the world.

The Snape Maltings Riverside Centre now boasts a wide range of shops including Craft, Antiques, House and Garden, Countrywear, Beachcomber, Books and Toys, and Maltings Music. Other facilities include self-catering accommodation, painting and craft courses, art exhibitions and the world famous Snape Maltings Concert Hall. One-hour river trips are available from April to October from the quay in a sheltered passenger boat, sailing down the River Alde's quiet estuary, renowned for colonies of avocet and shelduck.

Snape

The village of Snape attracts thousands of visitors to the maltings complex every year but there is more to the village than the maltings. Snape is also well known for the Anglo Saxon burial ships that have been discovered either side of the A1094 road. The site is east of the church and in 1862 Aldeburgh historian Septimus Davidson discovered a 14½ metre long burial ship.

The Walk

Starting from the maltings, cross Snape Bridge spanning the River Alde and take the river side path on the right along the banks of the river, opposite the Maltings Quay. Walk along this raised river bank path eastwards as it wends its way through the reeds and the quietness of the quite unspoilt country. Don't forget to bring your binoculars if you are a bird watcher, there will be plenty to see on this first section of the walk.

The path eventually rises into the trees and meets a crossing path, turn left through the woodland and look out for a left turn, where the path is marked with a waymark post. This path follows the right side of a marshy area, along a ditch and wire fence, and is called the Canser Path, an old Saxon word for a path avoiding flooding. At the end of the straight path turn right up the track to Priory Road.

Turn right along the road uphill through the bends to a track on the left marked with a bridleway sign. This is Guilding's Lane and leads between the houses and the playing field with a view of Snape Church ahead. The path soon becomes narrow at the playing field, but continues on to a left bend to emerge out to Church Road, by a red brick house with a fine pantile roof. Snape Church dates from the 13th and 15th centuries and is worth a detour from the walk, but

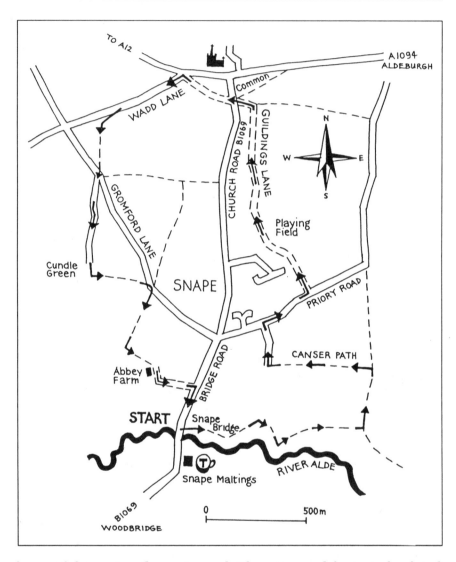

be careful crossing the main road. The octagonal font can be dated from around 1500.

Cross Church Road to the gravel track across Snape Common, following the fronts of the houses and out onto Wadd Lane. Turn left along the lane and walk as far as the first house and trees on the left. Turn left here, marked with a footpath sign behind a tree, to a stile at the back giving access to a cross field path. Follow this down to the right, heading for a pink thatched house at the bottom and passing an electricity pole in the middle of the field.

Cross Gromford Lane and walk down the lane opposite to Cundle Green. At the end of the lane continue straight on along a path through the trees marked with a footpath sign and then left up the side of a field, following the path out to Gromford Lane once again. Turn right for about 25 metres and then right at the first footpath, along a field edge path to the right of a hedge. This may become a little overgrown with lush growth in the summer but at the end of the hedge, just before the field corner, turn left, walking to the left of a newly planted hedge to Abbey Farm.

The fine 13th century barn was probably built by the monks of the Benedictine Priory, which was once situated between the farm and the river. At the end of the new hedge turn right onto the farm drive, following it past Abbey Farm House and out to Bridge Road. Turn right along the roadside footway to return to The Maltings at Snape Bridge.

Walk 24: Southwold

Route: Southwold Harbour – River Blyth – Walberswick Village –
Walberswick Church – Church Road – Southwold Railway – Buss Creek –
Southwold Pier and Promenade – Ferry Path – Southwold Harbour.

Terrain: Track, riverside path, road and former railway, 4 stiles.

Start: Southwold Harbour car park, Ordnance Survey map reference TM
504749.

Length: 6 miles (several short cuts).

Map: Ordnance Survey Pathfinder sheet 966 Southwold and Halesworth
(Explorer sheet 231).

Public Transport: For details telephone Suffolk County Council's Public
Transport Information TraveLine – 0645 583358.

Road Route: From A12 at Blythburgh take A1095 through Southwold to
the harbour. Pay and display parking available.

The Tea Shop

Squires, 71 High Street, Southwold. Telephone 01502 723354. Proprietors Gerald and Christine Sawyer. Traditional tea shop and restaurant, home made cakes and cream teas. Soups, snacks, lunches,
roast of the day and old fashioned puddings. Children's menu, licensed.

Opening times – 9am to 5pm Monday to Saturday (closed Wednes-
days from October to May), 12noon to 5pm Sundays. Specialty shop
with Swiss, German, Belgian and American chocolates.

Alternative tea shop – The Parish Lantern, Walberswick. Telephone 01502 723173. Open daily from 10am to 5pm, (Winter opening Friday, Saturday and Sunday only).

Southwold

Southwold has only one connecting road and is surrounded by
river, creek and sea, resulting in limited access, especially during
the summer months when many day trippers come to visit the town.
In 1659 a fire destroyed the town and little was saved except the me-

dieval church of St Edmund's. The white lighthouse, built in 1892, and church, dominate the town, which once had a flourishing harbour supporting a large fishing fleet. The town is now known mostly as a holiday resort and the home of Adnams Brewery who still use horse drawn drays to deliver the ale around the town.

Walberswick

Across the Harbour and the River Blyth is the village of Walberswick, once a prosperous settlement with an extensive fishing fleet and a large church. Henry VIII robbed the parish of its tithes in the 16th century and much of the fabric of the church was sold off to pay for the repair of public buildings after the town had become ruined and to rebuild a smaller church in 1695. There is no longer a fishing fleet and the village is now famous for its annual crabbing competition.

Walberswick – The Street

Southwold Railway

The railway ran through the Blyth valley between Southwold and Halesworth with the aim of developing the port of Southwold, and to and promote Southwold as a holiday resort. The railway brought about a considerable change in the development of the town as a result, a branch line was even built to the harbour on the north side. The coaches were small and open-ended with balconies and tram style seats facing each other down the sides. They ran on an unusual 3 foot gauge track at a maximum speed of 16mph, which proved a handicap when competing with improving road traffic. There were intermediate stations at Wenhaston and Walberswick Common, but the line finally closed on 20 April 1929.

The Walk

Start from the Harbour Car Park and follow the River Blyth inland along the road and rough track providing access to the facilities of a typical small harbour. In the summer take the Foot Ferry to the Walberswick side, the ferryman will skillfully row you quickly to the other side for a very small fee, even when the tide is racing in or out of the river. At other times, walk along the river side track and path, past the Harbour Inn, to the modern Bailey Bridge. Cross to the other side and return to the ferry landing stage by walking back along the footpath on the opposite bank.

From Walberswick Harbour follow The Street up through the village, taking care of the traffic as there is no roadside footway. At St Andrew's Church turn right on Church Road and at the end, continue on the track ahead, turning left through the gorse. Follow the path to the rear of an asbestos building and then along the left of a wire fence, through the gorse and open heathland.

The path eventually reaches the English Nature Walberswick Reserve and a seat. Turn right up onto the former track bed of the old Southwold to Halesworth railway. The track bed path is straight and level through a shallow cutting and curves left to Squires Hill, where the path joins a section of tarmac. Turn left to continue on across the modern Bailey Bridge over the River Blyth where the railway once crossed on a swing bridge.

At the other side, turn left over a stile onto the raised path on the embankment along Buss Creek, following the bank path out to the A1095 road at Mights Bridge. To avoid a number of stiles and for an easier walk, use the route of the former railway to rejoin the walk at Mights Bridge.

Before crossing the A1095, the only road into Southwold, note the fishing facility provided by the Southwold Angling Society for disabled people by Mights Bridge. Follow the embankment path past the Boating Lake to emerge at the Beach Car Park. At this point we join the Suffolk Coast and Heaths Path, stretching 50 miles from Lowestoft to Felixstowe along the Suffolk Heritage Coast.

Turn right through the car park and past the Pier, now considerably shortened since the days when paddle steamers called. Continue along the cliff top path past the Sailors Reading Room to Gun Hill, noting the former coastguard lookout which houses an RNLI Museum. Alternatively you may wish to wander through the town to seek refreshment, or use the promenade and beach for this section of the walk.

At Gun Hill turn right on the wide grass strip between the houses to the road and turn left to the Ferry Path, on the other side of the road after the junction with Gardner Road. To return to the Harbour you can either use this path with views across Town Marshes or wander through the Dunes behind the beach to return to the start of the walk at the Harbour car park.

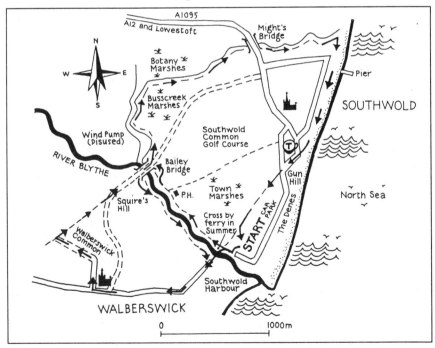

Walk 25: Stanton

Route: Stanton War Memorial – The Street – Bury Lane – Half Grove Wood – Wyken Road – Kiln Wood – Wyken Hall Farm – Rushgreen Grove – Posters Lane – Potash Farm – Readings Lane – Wash Lane – Upthorpe Road – Bury Road – Stanton Village.

Terrain: Track, field and roadside footway – 1 stile, sometimes muddy in parts.

Start: Stanton Village Centre, Ordnance Survey map reference TL 966735.

Length: 5 miles (several short cuts).

Map: Ordnance Survey Pathfinder sheet 1053 Stanton and Barnham (Explorer sheet 230A).

Public Transport: For details telephone Suffolk County Council's Public Transport Information TraveLine – 0645 583358.

Road Route: Stanton is 25 miles north east of Ipswich and 9 miles north east of Bury St Edmunds. From A14 at Woolpit north on A1088 to Ixworth and A143 (Diss) to Stanton. Free parking at Recreation Ground car park.

Tea Shop

Leaping Hare Café, Wyken Vineyards, Stanton, Bury St Edmunds IP31 2DW. Telephone 01359 250287. Proprietor Lady Carlisle. Morning coffee, Mocha Italian coffee in cafetieres or decaffeinated. Afternoon teas, Ceylon, Darjeeling, Earl Grey, Lapsang Souchong and herbal. Lunches and soft drinks. Home made cakes – specialities Wyken carrot cake, frosted chocolate cake, date and orange cake, fruit scones with home made jam and butter.

Opening hours – Thursday, Friday, Saturday and Sunday 10am to 6pm. Evenings – Thursday, Friday, and Saturday. Morning coffee 10am to 11.30am, afternoon teas 3.30pm to 5.45pm. Country Store, Country House, Gardens (not open on Saturdays) and Vineyards.

Stanton

The old trackways and roads which have been by-passed by modern traffic provide ideal access to the quieter parts of the countryside. The green lanes around Stanton formed part of an ancient transport system, in use before the age of steam and the motor car, connecting the hamlets and villages with the produce markets in the area. On this walk you will pass many interesting countryside features such as Wyken (pronounced Wicken) Hall Vineyards, Stanton Windmill, and evidence of a former wartime air base. The old drove roads and lanes are now deserted and used mainly for farm access, many of them have interesting names including Posters Lane, Packlose Lane, Kings Lane, Pig Lane and Wash Lane, their origins leave much to the imagination!

Stanton Windmill is open at all reasonable times by enquiring at the Mill House. Admission charges – adults £1.50 and children 3 – 17 years 20p. No unaccompanied children.

The Leaping Hare Café

Wyken Hall

This farming estate was once occupied by the Romans and is re-corded in the Domesday Book. The Elizabethan manor house is sur-rounded by four acres of gardens, including herb garden, knot garden, rose garden, kitchen garden, wild flower meadows, nuttery and a copper beech maze. There is also a walk to visit the vineyards, supplying the fruit used to produce Wyken wines, on sale in the Leaping Hare Country Store, situated inside a 400 year old barn.

The Walk

From the War Memorial at the village centre, walk along The Street and then right, opposite the Cock Inn, up Bury Lane, past Stanton Primary School. Continue along the lane, past the Bowls Club and speed de–restriction signs where the tarmac surface of the road is replaced by a stony track. After Doctors Hall and Stanton Manor the track becomes a green lane through Half Grove Wood.

Exit out onto Wyken Road and turn left past Kiln Wood, ignoring the turning to Stanton on the left, and continuing on towards Wyken Hall. At the first sharp right bend in the road, walk straight on along the track through Wyken Hall Farm, with the buildings on the right and Dovehouse Wood on the left. Wyken Hall's Leaping Hare restaurant, cafe and vineyards are on the other side of the buildings on the right and can be accessed by continuing along the road and then left along the hall drive.

Walk along the track straight through the farm and at a fork by the field, bear right on a muddy section of track around the right edge. At the far end of the field, follow the track left along the edge of Rushgreen Grove and then right between a hedge and the edge of the wood. This section is a little narrow in places and is sometimes muddy where it has been churned up by the horses.

At the end of the wooded section the path opens out into a wide grass lane called Posters Lane. Half way along there is a left turn where a short cut can be made back to Stanton along Packlose Lane if required. Continue on down Posters Lane to a junction at the bottom. Turn left on the wide grass track leading up past Potash Farm to reach Readings Lane, the road to Walsham-Le-Willows.

Turn left for a few yards and then left again through a gap in the trees, on a short section between wire fences. This leads to a galvanised bridleway gate and a well kept tree lined green lane beyond. Note the large mound to the right which was part of Stanton airfield, the large mounds of surplus soil on these airfields were usually used for ground testing the aircraft guns. Remnants of the former war time air base can be seen on various sections of this walk between here and Stanton Mill. The track soon enters a narrow section between hedges, trees and ditches and at the end, crosses a wide bridge to give access to a good field edge path straight ahead. There are some good views over the surrounding countryside from here, directly ahead on the horizon, the top of Stanton windmill can be seen above the trees.

Follow the field edge down to meet Wash Lane, a crossing track where you can either continue on a path across the field opposite or turn right to reach the Upthorpe Road. If you cross the field there is a stile as you reach the road, but whichever route you use, turn left at Upthorpe Road on the roadside footway towards Stanton.

Pass the windmill and walk down into Stanton, at the road junction turn left along Bury Road, past Foundry House, to return to the start of the walk at the war memorial in the village centre.

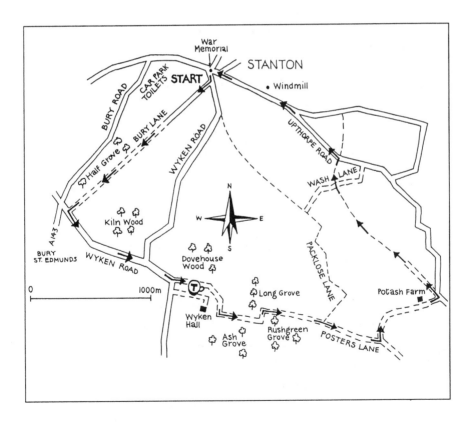

Walk 26: Thorpeness

Route: Thorpeness Meare – Windmill and House in the Clouds – Aldringham Common – Corporal's Belt Wood – Sizewell Hall – Sizewell Gap – Beach – Sizewell Cliffs – Beach – Thorpeness.

Terrain: Mainly tracks and well used paths, one cross field section, cliff top and beach, 2 stiles.

Start: The public car park at Thorpeness, Ordnance Survey map reference TM 472594.

Length: 5½ miles (several short cuts).

Map: Ordnance Survey Pathfinder sheet 1009 Aldeburgh and Orford (Explorer sheet 212).

Public Transport: For details telephone Suffolk County Council's Public Transport Information TraveLine – 0645 583358.

Road Route: From the A12 on A1094 Aldeburgh Road, turning north on B1069 and B1369 to Thorpeness. Pay and Display car park.

Tea Shop

The Gallery Coffee Shop, Remembrance Road , Thorpeness, Leiston IP16 4NW. Telephone 01728 453105. Proprietor John Strowger. Breakfasts, snacks, morning coffee, cappuccino coffee, lunches, afternoon teas, cream teas, gateaux. Food served all day, cod, plaice, scampi, jacket potatoes, lasagne, cottage pie, burgers, sausages, toasted sandwiches, salads, soups, daily specials. Take aways, ice creams, newspapers, milk, bread, eggs. Seating for 70, plus outside in enclosed garden, licensed.

Open every day 9am to 5pm and to dusk during the summer.

Alternative tea shop – Sizewell T at the beach car park, opening hours Wednesday to Sunday 9am to 5pm, closed in winter.

Thorpeness

Thorpeness was planned as a holiday village in 1910 and consists of many half timbered houses of all shapes and sizes. The House in the

Clouds is a converted water tank and with the Windmill as the pumping source, provided a water supply to the village. The Meare is a shallow artificial lake providing an ideal place for boating and very safe for children.

Sizewell

Sizewell Gap was once a small fishing haven and is still home to a number of fishing boats which can be seen winched up onto the shingle beach. The area was well known for its bands of organised smugglers, in 1745 as many as 300 horses and 100 carts were seen on the beach at one time, loading contraband goods for delivery throughout Suffolk.

The Walk

From the pay and display car park turn right along The Haven past the tea shop, the Meare and the end of Lakeside Avenue. Turn left on Uplands Road, a stony track signposted to Thorpeness Windmill. Continue on past the Windmill and the House in the Clouds to the golf club and look out for the path ahead through the gorse. Once out onto the open grass, follow the left edge of the golf course, along the hedge at the side of the Meare.

At the old Sheepgate railway crossing, on the former Leiston to Aldeburgh branch line,

The House in The Clouds, Thorpeness

cross over to a path to the left of the old gate into an area of heathland and wood. The path soon turns sharply right through the trees and then across a length of board walk and small bridge, following a line of electricity poles. After emerging out to a track turn right by a rail fence around a pine tree to a stile behind. This gives access out to a well defined cross field path, heading diagonally left towards the tallest tree and a stile on the other side. Walk between the gorse to reach a crossing track and turn right to reach the B1353 Thorpeness Road.

Cross straight over to a path through the gorse on the other side, following this through to meet a sandy track at a small clearing. Turn right on the track through the trees, passing the Providence Baptist Chapel and on round to a row of cottages. Turn right near the last house, on a path marked by a signpost, through the brambles, turn right after about 50 metres on a crossing path which becomes a track by the pine trees on the right.

Follow this sandy track to a fork at an open section then bear left to the route of the former railway, crossing where there was once a red brick overbridge. Continue on the other side to reach a junction of tracks. Turn left, now on a wide well used track, heading north east through the heathland. Keep to this track, bearing left at a fork, for about 1 mile, to reach a junction at the corner of the Sizewell Hall Estate.

Turn left following the boundary wall of the estate along the tree lined road with its chestnut trees, large pines and cypresses, passing the ornate iron gates, now disused and overgrown. Pass the main gates of Sizewell Hall, Home Farm and on to the main Sizewell to Leiston Road.

Turn right on the roadside footway, past the Vulcan Arms, following the road towards the car park and the beach. Turn right across the dunes on a boardwalk to the land behind the beach. Turn right by the public toilets, leaving Sizewell Nuclear Power station behind you. As you pass the fishing boats hauled up on the beach note the black boarded Coastguard Lookout, now manned only in emergencies. On the higher ground is a row of former coastguard cottages, and near the beach a wooden signal rocket pole. Continue south past the large white club house on the cliffs of Cliff House Caravan Site.

Just before you reach Sizewell Hall with its prominent chimneys, look for a waymark directing you up the steps in the cliff. Do not use the concrete steps with the green handrail a little further on which are private. At the cliff top turn left and walk between the walls of the grounds and the cliff and under the bridge.

Follow the flint wall past the raised Belvedere, which was used for admiring the fine coastal views. At the large concrete blocks, which were Second World War anti-tank defences, pause to appreciate the panoramic sea views of Sole Bay, Southwold Lighthouse can just be seen to the north.

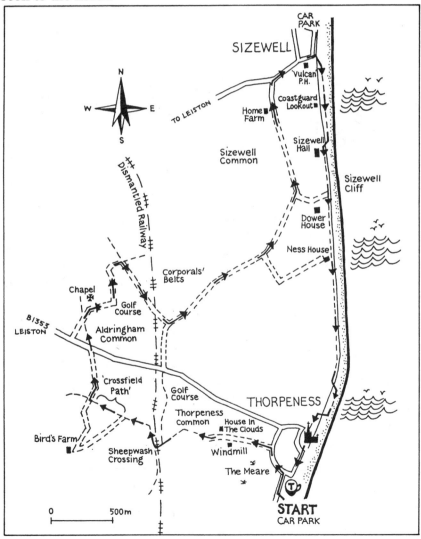

Sizewell beach

Continue along the cliff top or beach and on reaching the houses to the north of Thorpeness, turn left to the beach down some steps. Walk along the edge of the sand and shingle beach, here the fences of the houses come down to the edge of the beach and there is no alternative but to walk on the shingle for about 50 metres. Turn right through a wooden barrier on a path between the houses, to reach a short section of road.

Turn left at the end and, where the tarmac road bears right, turn left on Admiral's Walk, a stony track to The Heathlands. Turn right along the track, passing the rear of a grey church, to a tee junction on Church Road. Turn left and walk down the hill on Benthills, along the rear of the tea shop, to return to the start of the walk at the car park.

Walk 27: Wickham Market

Route: Market Hill – High Street – Walnuts Lane – Pettistree Church – Main Road – Loudham Lane – Ashe Abbey – The Oaks – River Deben – Fowls Watering – Mill Lane – Spring Lane – Wickham Market Church – Market Hill.

Terrain: Road, field edge and cross field, pasture and track, 8 stiles. Could be impassable in very wet weather if River Deben is in flood.

Start: Market Hill, Wickham Market, Ordnance Survey map reference TM 301558.

Length: 4 miles (several short cuts).

Map: Ordnance Survey Pathfinder sheet 1008 Wickham Market and Area (Explorer sheet 212).

Public Transport: For details telephone Suffolk County Council's Public Transport Information TraveLine – 0645 583358.

Road Route: Follow signs from the A12 Wickham Market by-pass to the village centre. Free car parking at Market Hill or off Church Lane.

Tea Shop

The Tea Pot Tearoom, 46 The Hill, Wickham Market IP13 0QS. Telephone 01728 748079. Proprietor Margaret Reeve. Pots of tea, Earl Grey, lemon and herbal. Freshly brewed coffee, decaffeinated coffee, hot chocolate, milk and a variety of soft drinks. Freshly cut sandwiches, home made cakes, cream teas, scones, toasted tea cakes, toast, sausage rolls. Jacket potatoes with various fillings, beans on toast, toasted sandwiches. All home made. Lunches served all day, soups, salads, daily luncheon specials on the board.

Opening hours – Monday to Saturday 9am to 5.30pm, Sunday (April to October) 10pm to 5pm. Seating for 25 plus 16 outside, no smoking. Collection of over 100 tea pots and an antique shop next door.

Wickham Market

The church of All Saints stands on a hill overlooking the River Deben with the 42 metre high spire dominating the skyline. The nearby

A12 dual carriageway now provides a by-pass for the town centre, which has returned to a quieter way of life. Although this was once a market town, today it retains the status of a village, albeit larger than the surrounding villages. The name Wickham is thought to come from the Roman word vicus or native settlement, established at the ford near the mill a the river, later becoming a trading place and eventually a market. By the time of the Domesday Book, the name of the town had changed to Wickham, although a chalice in the church dating from 1567 describes the village as Wiccom.

Pettistree

This country village is cosily tucked away off the beaten track and contains a mixture of thatched cottages and houses old and new, surrounding the church of St Peter and St Paul and the adjoining Greyhound pub. It is believed the pub, which backs on to the church yard, was built before the church and provided the builders with their refreshments.

The Tea Pot Tea Room, Wickham Market

Campsey Ash

Wickham Market railway station is actually in the nearby parish of Campsey Ash where the railway crosses the River Deben close to Ashe Abbey, the site of a former priory. Here the river runs through a large decoy pond, secluded amongst the trees, and once a valuable source of food for the table of the inhabitants of the priory.

The Walk

From Market Hill turn right along the High Street passing the church on the left and the Post Office on the right. After the large filling station and garage turn right on a path between conifer hedge and wall and then along a wide, well worn field edge path ahead to reach Walnuts Lane.

Turn left along the road to Pettistree Church which can be seen ahead. Turn left again through the gate by the tower and on to the path to the right of the church. Walk to the rear of the churchyard to a stile between pine trees leading out to a pasture beyond. Head for the unusual Rambler gate to the left of the steel gate ahead, and then in the next pasture, to the stile in the right corner, hidden behind the bushes.

Cross the next field, where the path should be well defined, to a gap in the fence and steps up to the main road. Cross the road with care to a stile on the other side and then on, straight ahead across the field, to a metal gate by an oak tree on the other side leading out to Loudham Lane.

Continue straight on along the road, crossing the A12 via an overbridge, past the gates to Loudham Hall and down into the River Deben valley. Just after Park Farm, by some white railings, there is a concrete footway on the left side, which can be used when the river is in flood. Continue round the bends and over the River Deben, there is a good view of Ashe Abbey and the Mill on the right and the decoy pond through a gap in the trees on the left.

Continue along the road to a red brick house on the right and take the stile in the rail fence opposite. Cross a short section of rough ground to a second stile and then up through the bracken and between the trees where the path follows a wire fence on the right. At the end of the fence continue on to a stile leading out to a field. Cross the field diagonally right to a gap in the hedge and out to the road.

Turn left for about 150 metres and then turn left through a gate into The Oaks. Follow the path down through the mixed woodland to another gate at the bottom. Cross the bridge with white railings ahead, over the River Deben, and on to a second bridge with white railings leading out to a wide field edge path.

Walk up the path on the right side of the field to the top and then turn right past the pink houses at Fowls Watering. Follow the access track round and then parallel to the A12 and then through an underpass to Mill Lane. Walk up the lane to the crossroads and turn right along Spring Lane.

At the top of the rise turn left over a high stile into a paddock and across to a second stile on the other side. The next section of path is a little narrow between fence and hedge and leads to a kissing gate at the field corner. Follow the path now between fences and hedges around left to a row of cottages. Turn right by No. 10, the first cottage in the row, on the path leading to the church. Walk through the churchyard and out to the High Street, turning right to return to the start of the walk at Market Hill.

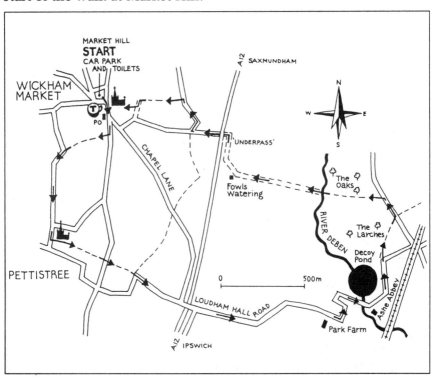

Walk 28: Woodbridge

Route: Woodbridge Station – Quay – River Deben – Melton Dock – Wilford Bridge – Melton Church – Woods Lane – Leeks Hill – Turnpike Lane – Sun Lane – New Street – Market Hill – Seckford Street – Fen Meadows – Warren Hill – Ipswich Road – Broomheath – Kyson Point – River Deben – Woodbridge Station.

Terrain: River wall path, track, road woodland and urban path, no stiles and easy walking.

Start: Woodbridge Station, Ordnance Survey map reference TM 273487.

Length: 6½ miles (several short cuts).

Map: Ordnance Survey Pathfinder sheets 1031 Woodbridge and 1008 Wickham Market and area (Explorer sheet 212).

Public Transport: For details telephone Suffolk County Council's Public Transport Information TraveLine – 0645 583358.

Road Route: From the A12 north of Ipswich and the Woodbridge by-pass, follow signs for Woodbridge Station (off Station Road/Quayside). Pay and Display car parks.

Tea Shop

The Whistle Stop Café and Restaurant, Old Station House, Station Road, Woodbridge IP12 4AU. Tel 01394 384381. Proprietor Sue Bell. Pots of tea, coffee, hot chocolate and wide range of cold drinks. Full English breakfast served all day. Wide range of hot and cold snacks, filled rolls, toasted sandwiches, filled jacket potatoes, specials on the blackboard. Home made cakes, scones, puddings and deserts. Children's menu, crisps and sweets. Lunches served between 12noon and 2.30pm. Seating for 25 plus outside seating in the summer. No smoking, wheelchair access.

Opening hours from Tuesday to Sunday 9am to 4pm, but later during the summer months. Bed and breakfast available.

Tide Mill

A mill was first recorded on this site in 1170 and is the last working tide mill in the country. It is one of the earliest tide mills to be recorded in Britain and even after the 56 centimetre square oak shaft of the water wheel broke, the mill continued to operate commercially under diesel power until 1957. The present building dates from 1793 and was restored and opened to the public in 1975. Now fully restored the mill operates from the reduced tidal pool at the rear, depending on the tides. The water from the incoming tide is stored in the mill pond and at low tide is released through the mill to turn the 5½ metre diameter undershot wheel for up to 1 hour.

Woodbridge Harbour and Tide Mill

The River Deben

Possibly the most picturesque and probably the most historically interesting of all the rivers of the East Coast, the River Deben rises near Debenham and flows through 32 miles of unspoilt Suffolk countryside to discharge into the North Sea at Felixstowe Ferry. The Wilford Bridge at Melton, just a mile or two upstream from Woodbridge, is the lowest road crossing point on the river. From here it is navigable to the sea and provides a wonderful tidal waterway for recreational boating, with craft of all shapes, sizes and colours to be seen. However, when reading about the River Deben, most writers describe the tidal river and could be led to believe that there was nothing above the Wilford Bridge. But the freshwater upper reaches of the river, meandering through the countryside of East Suffolk, are equally as picturesque as the tidal section that is so well known.

The Walk

From the railway station cross the railway line via the bridge on the left, next to the Riverside Theatre, to reach the river wall on the other side of the tracks. Turn left and follow the path on the edge of the dock to the Woodbridge Art Club on Tide Mill Way. Turn left through the flood protection gate and then immediately right on the path marked River Bank Path.

Where this becomes a track and comes out close to the railway, turn down the path by the Woodbridge Boat Store marked with white posts, and follow the path parallel to the river, by a black boarded fence, to regain the river wall. Follow the river side path around Melton Dock and on past the Melton Picnic Site to exit to the road at the Wilford Bridge.

Cross the road to the tarmac track opposite and walk to the railway crossing, taking care to Stop Look and Listen before crossing. Continue along the track, keeping to the left of the conifer hedge to reach the woods ahead. Turn left along the edge of the wood, following the track along the backs of the houses. At the end of the fence on the left, turn left off the track, continuing with the fence and houses on the left to reach the road close to Melton's St Andrew's Church.

Turn right on the roadside footway to The Street at the Horse and Groom pub. Turn left through the village to the traffic lights at the cross roads and turn right up Woods Lane. Just after the Valley Farm Road, turn left up Leeks Hill, by a red post box in the wall. Where the drive turns sharply right, continue straight on down into the trees through a metal barrier. Continue along this undulating path through the wood, ignoring any side turnings to reach a path junction marked with a footpath sign. Turn left down the path in the gully to exit through a metal barrier on to Turnpike Lane, a stony track that was probably once an important road.

Turn right and, just before a house called Pembertons, turn right through a staggered metal barrier, leading to a secluded footpath up through the trees. When the path emerges at the road, cross straight

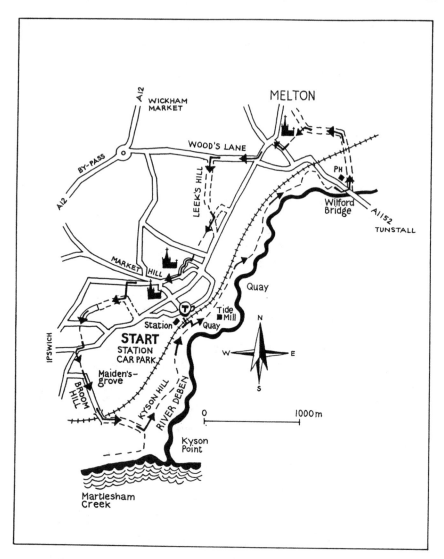

over and take the surfaced path (Adam's Walk), at the side of a red brick wall, to Sun Lane. At the lane turn right and then left on to St John's Hill, passing St John's church on the right, and down towards the town. At the T-junction turn right on New Street, noting Bridewell, one of the few exposed timber framed buildings in Woodbridge and then the Olde Bell and Steelyard. The overhanging projection or steelyard was used to weigh loaded carts, continue on to reach Market Hill.

Turn right up the hill and look out for the building on the right with the initials EFG over the door. This is where Edward Fitzgerald lived from 1860 to 1873, he is buried at nearby Boulge Church. Walk up around the Shire Hall, which was built, to house the court sessions, the ground floor was also once used as a corn market.

Walk to the top of Market Hill and to the left of the King's Head Inn, continue along Seckford Street. At the end of the houses on the left, turn left down some steps to Fen Meadows, following the path along the left edge. At the end of the chain link fencing, bear right up a sunken lane between hedges, emerging alongside the cemetery railings to reach Portland Crescent.

Follow the road down and then up to the junction with Warren Hill and cross to the path opposite between houses Nos. 25 and 27. Follow this between the garden fences to reach a set of steps down to a metal barrier on the Ipswich Road. Turn right along the roadside footway and then left along Sandy Lane, turning left again at a telephone kiosk, up a short section of stony drive, and then bearing left along the path at the side of the Woodland Trust's woods.

Where the path emerges onto Broomheath, continue on up the hill, passing the public car park on the right to reach the red brick railway bridge. Follow the stony track across the bridge and left down towards the river at Kyson Point. Turn left along the river wall path towards Woodbridge, following the river wall past the boat yards and sailing clubs to the Quay. Turn left up over the footbridge across the railway at Woodbridge Station to return to the start of the walk.

Walk 29: Woolpit

Route: Woolpit Church – Lady's Well Pocket Park – Old Stowmarket Road – Woolpit Green – Green Road – Deadman's Lane – Rags Lane – Village Centre.

Terrain: Road, track and field path, no stiles, muddy when wet.

Start: Woolpit village car park opposite St Mary's Church, Ordnance Survey map reference TL 975624.

Length: 3½ miles.

Map: Ordnance Survey Pathfinder sheet 984 Bury St Edmunds and Woolpit Explorer sheet 211A).

Public Transport: For details telephone Suffolk County Council's Public Transport Information TraveLine – 0645 583358.

Road Route: From Ipswich (18 miles) or Bury St Edmunds (7 miles) on A14 to junction with A1088, follow signs to Woolpit and the free car park opposite the church.

Tea Shop

Elm Tree Gallery, The Old Bakery, The Street, Woolpit, Bury St Edmunds IP30 9QG. Telephone and fax 01359 240255. Proprietor Anne Wilding. Teas, coffees, scones, tea cakes and various cakes. High quality gifts and crafts, some from far flung corners of the world, including tea pots from the birthplace of the teapot in the village of Yixing in China. Ceramics, glass, an extensive range of jewellery, greeting cards and gift stationery. Only two tables available and seating for up to ten people, seating outside on fine days. No smoking.

Opening hours – every day from 10am to 6pm except Sunday 2pm to 5pm. Immediately opposite is the Woolpit Local History Museum which is open from Easter to September 2.30pm to 5pm on Saturday, Sunday and Bank Holidays.

Woolpit

As you drive along the A14 trunk road towards Bury St. Edmunds the spire of Woolpit's 12th century flint Church of St Mary stands guard, looking out over the trees, inviting travellers to stop their journey and have a look round the old village. Woolpit is now off the route of the main road and the village is a quiet, welcoming place, with a car park opposite the church and several shops, pubs, tea shop and fish and chips for refreshment. It is also a historic village, in Lady's Well Park is a half moated site where pilgrims in the Middle Ages once stopped to bath their eyes in the water, reputed to have healing qualities, as they travelled to Walsingham. It is thought to be the site of the medieval chapel of Our Lady of Woolpit. The site is listed as an ancient monument and cared for by the local community.

There is a local legend that around 1400, two green children mysteriously appeared in a harvest field, a brother and sister who would only eat green beans. They were cared for and weaned off the beans by Sir Richard de Calne and although the boy later died, it appears the girl grew up, lost her green complexion and married a man from Kings Lynn.

Village pump, Woolpit

The Walk

From the car park cross the road to Rectory Lane, between the telephone kiosk and the church. At the first junction take the right fork towards the playing field and, where the tarmac ends, bear right to the main road. Turn right along the roadside verge until you reach Lady's Well Pocket Park on the opposite side of the road.

Cross to the gate by the Armada beacon and enter through the small gate to the left, there is a bolt on the inside securing the gate. The ancient Holy Well in the park is a scheduled ancient monument and is maintained by the village local history group. To explore the park follow the path around the old moated site, there are information boards describing the history and many of the tree species are named with small plaques, all providing an interesting feature to the walk.

Exit from the park where you came in and turn left on the roadside verge, passing a Tourist Information board on the way to the crossroads. Turn left on Old Stowmarket Road, the old route of the main road into the village, using the roadside footway which lines the route for most of the way. After passing a large pond on the right and at the end of the footway, turn right where it is marked with a footpath sign, on the access drive through Swan Lake Brickworks. There are several old clay pits in the area which since around 1500 have provided the material for a thriving brick making industry.

Where the drive turns sharply left at the end, continue straight on across the grass, marked with a yellow waymark arrow on a post. Walk through the trees and then on across a section of arable field to the corner of the hedge ahead. Continue on the grassy track on the other side of the field to reach Heath Road.

Turn left along the road, beware of fast moving traffic, it is safest to walk on the right facing the oncoming traffic except at bends, where it is safer to walk on the outside of the bend in order that drivers will see you earlier. At the first junction turn right, signposted to Woolpit Green. At the road junction in Woolpit Green there is a surfaced path on the right providing a short cut back to the village if required. For the main walk continue straight on along Green Road, passing Grange Farm, and as far as the next junction, signposted Drinkstone 1½ miles.

Turn left down the hill and, at the bottom after crossing the bridge with white railings, turn left up the lane as far as the first sharp left

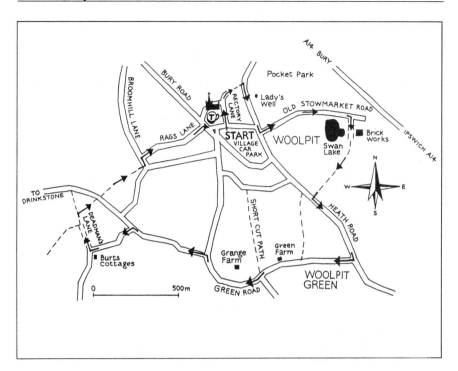

bend by a pair of houses. Turn right on Deadmans Lane, a grassy track which narrows and becomes bounded bv hedges. Look out for a yellow waymark arrow in the trees showing a right turn across an arable field, follow this out to the road.

Cross the road to the path marked with a footpath sign and between fences, then out on an unploughed strip up across the fields towards the houses ahead. At the road turn left for a short way and then right on Rags Lane, following this to emerge in the village on Bury Road.

Turn right to the pump in the village centre where there are several shops and pubs for refreshment. Follow the road round to the left past the Old Bakery and tea shop towards the church and the start of the walk at the car park opposite.

```
┌─────────────────────────────────────────────────────────┐
│                                                         │
│              Walk 30: Wortham                           │
│                                                         │
└─────────────────────────────────────────────────────────┘
```

Route: Wortham Post Office – Long Green – Open Field – Church Road – Wortham Church – Hall Farm – Open Field – The Marsh – Wortham Common.

Terrain: Field edge, pasture, cross field, track and road, 4 stiles.

Start: Wortham Post Office Stores, Ordnance Survey map reference TM 086772.

Length: 3½ miles (two short cuts).

Map: Ordnance Survey Pathfinder sheet 964 Diss (South) and Botesdale (Explorer sheet 23A).

Public Transport: For details telephone Suffolk County Council's Public Transport Information TraveLine – 0645 583358.

Road Route: Wortham is on the A143 Bury St. Edmunds to Diss road, 3 miles west of Diss and 4 miles north east of Eye.

Tea Shop

The Olde Tea Shoppe, The Post Office Stores, Wortham, Diss, Norfolk IP22 1PP. Telephone 01379 783210. Proprietors Alison and Leslie Dumbell. Pots of tea, coffee, chocolate, soft drinks, licenced. Extensive all day menu, sandwiches, home made cakes and cream teas, scones, toasted tea cakes, ice creams. Savouries, jacket potatoes, lunches and salads, lasagne, home made steak and kidney and cottage pies, fish.

Opening hours – all week 9am to 7pm throughout the summer and 9am to 6pm in winter. Closed all day Sunday and Tuesday in January and February. Seating for 50+, parties up to 50 by arrangement. Children welcome, disabled access, tea garden. Ample parking space. Crafts, pottery, plants, local wines, books, garden ornaments and plants. The tea shop is in an Elizabethan hay barn adjoining the Post Office Stores, set back from the main road across the common land.

Wortham Commons

The area of north Suffolk close to the Norfolk border abounds in patches of common land or greens dotted across the landscape. With the neighbouring parish of Burgate, the two villages include a large number of these sites. Burgate has its Great and Little Greens whilst in Wortham there is Long Green and The Marsh, both of which are designated County Wildlife Sites and Wortham Ling, which is a Site of Special Scientific Interest (SSSI). Close to the village centre Long Green is acidic grassland and is managed in a variety of ways, it is noted for the many ponds, often surrounded by bramble and scrub. The Marsh, as the name suggests, is a low lying area of wet land with patches of drier ground providing a habitat to support a wide range of wildlife. To the north of the parish, Wortham Ling is managed by the Suffolk Wildlife Trust as a nature reserve and is a mixed area of woodland, heath and grass open to the public for walking.

Wortham Church and Watch Tower

Wortham Church

The church of Saint Mary's consists of the main church and the remains of a large round tower. The original church is believed to date from around 1160 and was rebuilt in 1360, but the tower is thought to be have been built as a watch tower and was standing before the church was built. This tower is the largest round flint church tower in the country and is 9 metres in diameter, originally 19 metres high and contained 4 bells. The roof and upper floors of the tower collapsed in 1789 and the bells were sold by the parish. Of particular interest inside are the finely sculptured pew ends. These are carved from oak, seasoned in the parish, and depict animals and people illustrating the words of Psalm 104, each with an appropriate inscription carved below.

The Walk

From the Post Office Stores turn right along the A143 towards Bury St. Edmunds on the roadside footway. Turn right at Church Road and then diagonally left across the grass to the Redgrave Road and Long Green. After passing an open pond on the left at about 800 metres, turn right on a stony track with a sign to Spring Field. Take the grassy opening between the houses and then a narrow path between rail fence and ditch to reach a railway sleeper bridge leading into the next field.

Turn right along a field edge path with the hedge on the right, and after about 300 metres, look out for another small bridge across the ditch to the field on the other side. Turn left along this wide field edge, now with the hedge and ditch on the left, following the path through a number of fields and out to Church Road. Turn left along the road, taking great care of the fast traffic on the bends, to reach the junction at Wortham Church.

Walk up through the churchyard and bear to the right of the church building to a kissing gate at the rear, leading out to a pasture. Bear diagonally right to a stile and concrete bridge, and then on to another stile in the corner by a gate. Climb the second stile behind this and walk up the wide grass path, at the side of a young plantation, to the top of the hill. At the top continue straight across the arable field ahead, making for a point to the left of the thatched cottage on the other side. As you cross there is an excellent view to the left of the River Waveney valley and the county of Norfolk on the other side. The path passes through a tiled car port and down the drive of the cottage to the road.

Turn right along the road to a tee junction and take the track practically opposite. This is muddy to start and then becomes grass until it reaches a field boundary. The public right of way now crosses four arable fields, for guidance look out for a line on the ground, a gap in a hedge and a small bridge with steps. Finally, head for a pink house on the other side of the final field. Cross the stile and footbridge into the garden, then bear right past the end of the pink house and out to the access track through the garden gate. Follow the track through The Marsh and out to the main A143 road. Turn right along the roadside footway to return to the start of the walk at the Post Office Stores and Olde Tea Shoppe on Long Green.

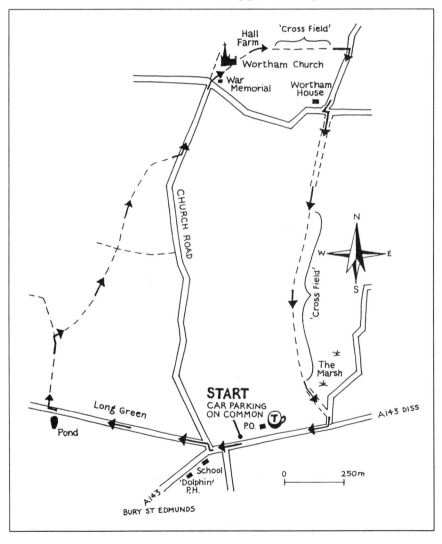

Tea Shop Walks - Spreading everywhere!

The Sigma Leisure Tea Shop Walks series already includes:

Cheshire

The Chilterns

The Cotswolds

The Lake District, Volume 1

The Lake District, Volume 2

Lancashire

Leicestershire & Rutland

North Devon

The Peak District

Shropshire

Snowdonia

South Devon

Staffordshire

Surrey & Sussex

Warwickshire

The Yorkshire Dales

Each book costs £6.95 and contains an average of 25 excellent walks: far better value than any other competitor!

In case of difficulty, or for a free catalogue, please contact: **SIGMA LEISURE, 1 SOUTH OAK LANE, WILMSLOW, CHESHIRE SK9 6AR.** Phone: 01625-531035 Fax: 01625-536800. E-mail: sigma.press@zetnet.co.uk . Web site: http//www.sigmapress.co.uk

VISA and MASTERCARD orders welcome. Please add £2 p&p to all orders.

 MAGAZINE

 EVENTS

 COMPETITIONS

 MEMBER DISCOUNTS

Tea is our most social and sociable drink – a part of our national heritage and daily life for well over 300 years. The Tea Club exists so its members can share and enjoy the history, traditions and romance associated with this fascinating drink.

 TASTINGS & SAMPLING

 A FREE GIFT WHEN YOU JOIN

THERE'S SO MUCH MORE
TO TEA THAN JUST
A CUPPA !

HOW TO JOIN

Simply send your name, full address and postcode to:

The Tea Club

PO Box 221

Guildford, Surrey GU1 3YT

and an application form will be sent to you immediately.

Tea Club Memberships are also a great gift idea – why not send one to a friend !

TSW/1